"In this delightful and practical book, Cindy Bunch offers creative—even playful—ideas for cultivating awareness about the things that provoke us and bring us joy. *Be Kind to Yourself* is a generous invitation to relax into the grace of God and embrace a posture of compassionate curiosity rather than self-condemnation. I'm grateful for Cindy's wisdom and transparency and will read and recommend this book again and again."

Sharon Garlough Brown, author of the Sensible Shoes series

"'What's bugging you? What's bringing you joy?' With these two simple questions, Cindy Bunch, like an experienced mariner, masterfully steers us through the choppy seas of negative self-talk and disheartening feelings that we all know so well. Each chapter of *Be Kind to Yourself* is a testimony to an important insight: by responding to God's grace with classic spiritual practices, we can anchor our lives in a peaceful harbor resplendent with joy and free of frustrations. This is wise and practical spiritual formation at its best!"

Albert Haase, OFM, author of *Becoming an Ordinary Mystic*

"All too often we are focused on the highs and lows of life, which may be less than 20 percent of our days. But how can we enjoy the plain, old, routinely typical day? Thanks, Cindy, for inviting us to see and know the presence of God in the ordinary days of our lives and helping us to hold on to the 'unforced rhythms of grace.' May *Be Kind to Yourself* become a go-to for all who long to stay awake to the beauty and revelations of life."

Juanita Campbell Rasmus, spiritual director, copastor of St. John's United Methodist Church, Houston, and author of *Learning to Be*

"*Be Kind to Yourself* is bo'   ᵈ confessional. An array of old and
new practices helps the   questions.
Stories of her own faithfᵤ   be gentle
with ourselves in the cʰ   ʰat Cindy
offers is an honest, doaˡ   D1472674   and self."

Sybil MacBeth, author of *Pra...*

"*Be Kind to Yourself* is chock full of essential truths and insights, and creative, empowering, and practical tools. As a writer, counselor, and spiritual director, I was challenged and encouraged by this book to be more gentle with myself and others. I believe it will do the same for any small group, retreat, book club, or individual wanting to more fully embrace joy. This book is a treasure trove that you will return to again and again."

Sheila Wise Rowe, counselor, spiritual director, and author of *Healing Racial Trauma* and *The Well of Life*

"I sometimes say unkind things to myself that I would never say out loud to another person. We really do need to learn to be kind to ourselves as God is kind to us. *Be Kind to Yourself* is a beautiful and practical guide to show us how. Thank you for sharing your wisdom, Cindy."

Alan Fadling, president of Unhurried Living and coauthor of *What Does Your Soul Love?*

"Reading this book is like taking a walking tour of real life at ground level and making the surprising discovery that each day's prickly pokes and elegant graces are fodder for meaningful engagement with life and God. Cindy Bunch, in her marvelous book *Be Kind to Yourself*, shares her own story with candid vulnerability, stopping along the way to illustrate and introduce creative and livable spiritual practices. This book is truly a gem, and from an author who embodies its truths artfully and authentically. You will love it!"

Beth A. Booram, director of Fall Creek Abbey, coauthor of *When Faith Becomes Sight*

"Cindy Bunch's wise new book shows us how to extend the same compassion to ourselves that we've all been taught to give to others. It's a self-kindness rooted in the affection and attention of a God who is simply wild about us. I wish I'd had this book twenty-five years ago. I'm grateful to have it now."

John Pattison, coauthor of *Slow Church*

BE KIND
TO
Yourself

RELEASING FRUSTRATIONS
AND EMBRACING *Joy*

CINDY BUNCH

FOREWORD BY RUTH HALEY BARTON

An imprint of InterVarsity Press
Downers Grove, Illinois

InterVarsity Press
P.O. Box 1400, Downers Grove, IL 60515-1426
ivpress.com
email@ivpress.com

InterVarsity Press® is the book-publishing division of InterVarsity Christian Fellowship/USA®, a movement of students and faculty active on campus at hundreds of universities, colleges, and schools of nursing in the United States of America, and a member movement of the International Fellowship of Evangelical Students. For information about local and regional activities, visit intervarsity.org.

All Scripture quotations, unless otherwise indicated, are taken from The Holy Bible, New International Version®, NIV®. Copyright © 1973, 1978, 1984, 2011 by Biblica, Inc.™ Used by permission of Zondervan. All rights reserved worldwide. www.zondervan.com. The "NIV" and "New International Version" are trademarks registered in the United States Patent and Trademark Office by Biblica, Inc.™

While any stories in this book are true, some names and identifying information may have been changed to protect the privacy of individuals.

Cover design and image composite: Cindy Kiple
Interior design: Jeanna Wiggins
Images: colorful bug illustrations: © mustafahacalaki / DigitalVision Vectors / Getty Images
       floral illustration: © awardik / DigitalVision Vectors / Getty Images
Author photo on back cover: Rebekah Byrd

ISBN 978-0-8308-4676-4 (print)
ISBN 978-0-8308-4677-1 (digital)

Printed in the United States of America ♾

Library of Congress Cataloging-in-Publication Data
A catalog record for this book is available from the Library of Congress.

P 25 24 23 22 21 20 19 18 17 16 15 14 13 12 11 10 9 8 7 6 5 4 3 2 1

Y 41 40 39 38 37 36 35 34 33 32 31 30 29 28 27 26 25 24 23 22 21 20

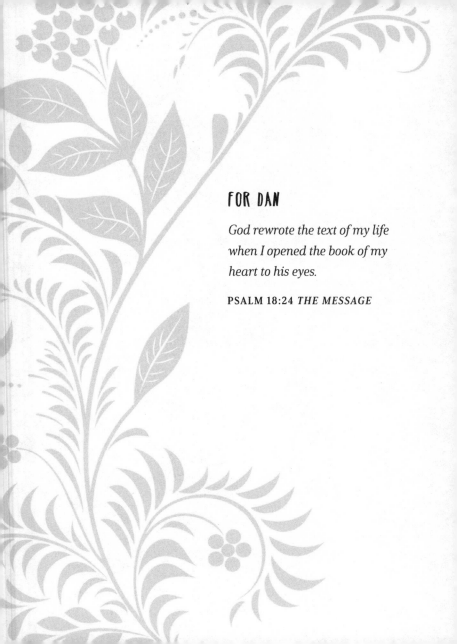

FOR DAN

God rewrote the text of my life when I opened the book of my heart to his eyes.

PSALM 18:24 *THE MESSAGE*

CONTENTS

FOREWORD

Ruth Haley Barton

"The only true gift is a portion of oneself" writes Ralph Waldo Emerson, and this, to me, is an apt description of what Cindy has done in the book you hold in your hand. She has shared with us generous portions of herself—her own story, her honest struggles, and the practices that have helped her endure and find joy in the midst of it all. Since all of us have our own stories that include joy and pain, gladness and sadness, this is something we all need.

I love that this book is ordered around the general practice of self-kindness, an idea we hear very little about these days and yet is sorely needed. Most of us have lived so long in highly judgmental and overly evaluative environments, we might wonder if self-kindness is even allowed. But the truth is if we just learned how to practice this, we would be changed! And, as Cindy so wisely points out, so would our relationships, because being tender with ourselves begets tenderness and consideration toward others.

This book is deeply encouraging because it offers us small, simple practices that can have a big impact if we let them. From the shame-free examen to the visio divina walk to the songs that bring you joy playlist or even the practice of smashing things (!) to release grief and anger, this work offers a plethora of practices that require nothing more than shifting our focus and recalibrating our thoughts, attitudes, and intentions for loving and spiritual purposes. Cindy's intimate and fresh insights, combined with specific and concrete practices, make for wise spiritual guidance.

A very personal joy for me in perusing this book is Cindy's reflections on the practice of spiritual direction in general and the impact of Marilyn Stewart's life and ministry specifically. In Marilyn I found a cherished spiritual friendship that spanned over twenty years as well as a role model who continually inspired my own ministry. Reading Cindy's reflections on what Marilyn meant to her during a harrowing season of her own journey is a great gift to all of us who knew and loved Marilyn.

Finally, I am convinced that the art, photography, and creative exercises woven as a thread throughout this work will be a blessing to many—including (and maybe even most especially!) those who do not think of themselves as creative or artistic. Since we are all made in the image of the One who created and is creating, there is something in each of us that is capable of giving ourselves over to the creative process as one aspect of being in relationship with our creator God. My hope is that all who find themselves with this book in their hands will engage the practices—all of them—including the ones that involve art and creativity. I pray you will be kind to yourself *and* stretch yourself. I promise, you won't regret it!

INTRODUCTION

What's Bugging You?

"Notice when you are bugged." That statement stopped me short as I was reading. The things that bug me can form a low hum in my brain throughout a day. They can spoil—or threaten to spoil—the other lovely moments of the day.

I found these words in the manuscript for Gem and Alan Fadling's book *What Does Your Soul Love?* in a section where they were describing how we place ourselves in a state of openness before God. In my work as an editor, I get to read wonderful books and interact with some very wise souls. When I am reading in manuscript form, I am often in professional mode, thinking of the structure of the book, how the audience will receive it, and so on. But sometimes a line or section jumps out to me. Then I know *those words are for me.* It is God offering me a nudge in the midst of the workday.

I took that statement and made it into a question. Then I decided to make it a part of a daily practice. I would think about the past day and write down the answer to just two questions:

1. What's bugging you?
2. What's bringing you joy?

Creating that simple practice has been a great help to me. As I lean into it, I see where I am hooked into negative thought patterns about myself or others and recognize what I need to let go of. I also see what brings me joy. And each day brings a new opportunity to lean into that as well. The more I understand about what's bugging me and free myself of that, the more I am able to embrace opportunities for joy. It's part of what I am learning about being kind to myself.

SELF-KINDNESS

The ways that we talk to ourselves about the things that are bugging us are a part of a practice of self-kindness. What do I say to myself when what's bugging me is the way that I escalated a small matter into a situation where I yelled at my husband? How do I process those moments when I am passed over at work? Or when a friend makes a hurtful comment? Or even something as mundane as getting stuck in an hour-long customer service call with no satisfaction?

> "No life of faith can be lived privately. There must be overflow into the lives of others."
> EUGENE PETERSON

As we learn new ways of dealing with the moments of difficulty in each day, we make space for the moments of joy to take greater hold of us.

Scripture tells us to "love your neighbor as yourself" (Mark 12:31). And we may have even heard it noted in a sermon that we should not neglect ourselves as we care for others. But often that is simply said in passing as we focus on being of service to the world. Giving our attention to what it means to love ourselves may feel selfish. Yet even Jesus took time away from the crowds he was teaching to pray (Luke 5:16).

Another benefit of this increased self-kindness is that when we are tender with ourselves, we cultivate a greater tenderness and empathy toward others. It is a fruit of goodness to ourselves that we increase in goodness toward our neighbor. Anne Lamott describes how she learned from others who were getting sober that "extending ourselves to others would help us stay sober and sane." The pattern of getting a sponsor in AA follows this principle. But then Lamott continues, "They also wanted us to extend ourselves to our own horrible selves, at our most ruined, to speak gently to ourselves, get ourselves a lovely cup of tea." For many of us, offering grace to ourselves is harder than extending grace to others.

Over time I have discovered practices that have helped me to identify and work with the daily pain I carry and also to embrace the things that bring me awareness of God's very good gifts. These practices are recorded here in hopes that they will assist others in the journey into deepening joy—not to be a guilt-inducing catalog of things to do. Read and practice at your own pace. Pick up the practices that you are drawn to and let the others go in keeping with Jesus' offer of "unforced rhythms of grace" (Matthew 11:29 *The Message*).

SHAME-FREE EXAMEN

I have long struggled with the traditional understanding of how to practice examen, a pattern of prayer that comes from Saint Ignatius, the sixteenth-century mystic and founder of the Jesuits. The basic idea is to take a bit of time in the evening to sit and mentally review the day—play it through like a movie. As you do so, notice where you felt close to God (moments of consolation), and notice where you felt far from God (moments of desolation). To me, this practice always felt like another way to feel bad about myself—a way to review and recall all of my sin for the day. While I know it's good to remember my sin so that I can confess it to God, the review would throw me into a place of shame. Further, doing it at night reminded me of all the things I could be worrying over just as I was trying to go to sleep. For me, it was not a good combination.

Using these two simple daily review questions took the edge off the pain and made the practice more accessible to me. A further tweak for me was to review the previous day in the morning. I was already in a morning routine of spiritual reading and journaling, so it fit right in. I spend a few moments thinking about the day that has passed. Then I write in my journal the answers to the two questions numbered with a 1 and a 2.

For a season I had a thirty-day booklet in which I wrote down the answers to my two questions. Each day I pasted in an image clipped out of magazine pages to represent one or both of my responses. (I keep a little stash of evocative magazine images—more about this can be found in the description of collage practice, chapter seven.) This gave me something tactile to do as I mused on the day and allowed me to focus more deeply. Finding the images drew out different aspects of what I was feeling.

PRACTICE: A DAILY RECORD

Commit to thirty days of recording the answers to these two questions:

1. What's bugging you?
2. What's bringing you joy?

You can list these in the space provided in this book. You can record them in a special notebook. Or you can just write it in a journal you already keep. There's a printable on the book page at ivpress.com/be-kind-to-yourself that you can download if you would like more space to write or would like to add art from magazines or your own illustration. Having this daily record to review will help you with some of the practices later in the book. If asking yourself, "What is bugging me?" doesn't resonate with you, you could try asking yourself, "What is frustrating me?" instead.

Tackling the examen from the approach of what's bugging me and what's making me happy keeps me out of the sinkhole of shame. The things that bug me are—of course—not completely outside myself. The truth is that things that bug me the most are often the personal encounters that go wrong. Or they may be things that are causing me worry or anxiety, running a never-ending mental loop. My part in it is my own response—whether simply internal or expressed.

These questions have made me more aware of the things I hold on to each day. The things that pull me down. The things that keep me from noticing that God is near and is constantly drawing me in.

IT'S THE LITTLE THINGS

Some of us may be in the habit of pushing down negative thoughts and so may not be readily aware of anything bugging us. This simple practice offers a way to get in touch with the idea that we are holding on to pain, frustration, and anger, so that we can work with them together with God.

Each chapter begins with what's bugging me. The illustrations come from various moments throughout my life, from the mundane workday to some dark periods of desolation to some embarrassing and painful failures. The things that bug me often stem from negative thinking and self-doubt. I explore spiritual practices that I have found can offer help and support in these areas.

While I do share some stories from a difficult part of my life, this book is primarily designed as a companion for ordinary days. When we are in times of intense grief and loss, the pain is with us all the time, coloring everything. What I've noticed for myself is that in these seasons the things that usually bug me don't bother me at all. When a loved one has recently died, an impatient clerk at the grocery store doesn't much penetrate the mental and emotional fog. In such a season everything is different.

It could be that some of the things that bug us are signs of underlying mental health issues; in this process you might find that themes emerge that can be explored in professional counseling. But those are not the themes that I am primarily attempting to address. In these pages we will focus on exploring the spiritual landscape of our lives.

After I've looked at what's bugging me, I can step back and see what brings me joy. I'm noticing everyday occurrences: The moment when someone spoke to me with kindness. Or helped me out with a task at work. The sunset on the drive home. The dinner my husband cooked for me.

I focus on the word *joy* in my daily practice rather than happiness because I believe that joy points to the deeper things that come from God. We know that happiness can be fleeting. Brother David Steindl-Rast writes, "Ordinary happiness is based on happenstance. Joy is that extraordinary happiness that is independent of what happens to us. Good luck can make us happy, but it cannot give us lasting joy." As I reflect on this statement, I think of the common story of lottery winners experiencing the same or a lowered level of happiness after winning.

Joy comes from the fruit of the Spirit—peace, patience, kindness, goodness, faithfulness, and (darn it) self-control. But I also like to have fun with identifying joy. I can record some little thing that just made me smile that day—like the knitting gnome GIF that I found and shared with some friends in a text. These things, too, can draw us to God.

Patterns of happiness will emerge over time and may point to needed life changes. The goal of this book, however, is to reveal ways that we can begin making tiny adjustments to our daily routines to let in more of the things that make us joyful. It's a matter of cultivating gratitude for the many reminders of God that we can find in an ordinary day. I offer some practices that I both intentionally and intuitively cultivated in my life. They are the things that consistently bring me joy.

Driving at rush hour and going to the DMV will always be unpleasant. But—sometimes—the pattern of what's bugging us points us to a deeper work that God is doing in us. Thus we find the first invitation from God in the very frustrations we experience. Noticing what's bugging us may be an opportunity to let go of some expectations we are holding on to and step into a new way of being. Then we turn toward cultivating joy. Because life is all mixed up like that—the good and the bad mingle together. As we pay attention to God's daily presence near us, we discover the antidote to what's bugging us. That's why the second invitation is to notice the daily moments of joy.

DISCOVER WHAT YOU KNOW

After years of experiencing spiritual direction with a wise and skilled director, I was privileged go through spiritual direction training myself. What I've found to be true as a spiritual director is that I'm not directing anything! I am just sitting with another person listening for the movement of the Holy Spirit within them. If a person is actively seeking God and pursuing spiritual practice, then most of the time, with a few probing questions, they are able to find the answers to their own questions. Spiritual direction is like talking with a close friend. You talk around all sides of a question together until you find your way to the center.

The process I'm inviting you into in these pages is like that. It's an opportunity to surface what you already know. To discover what you are already doing—or could be doing!—that brings you near to God. I'm intentionally not pushing forward a lot of content as most of us have more information coming at us than we can handle. Here's a space to focus on practice and experience.

Each chapter breaks down into smaller chunks with visual stopping points. Read a section at a time and try a practice—perhaps one a day or a week. Then return to reading the chapter. But remember, there's no need to feel compelled to try all the practices.

Another way to tackle the chapters would be to read the whole chapter, noticing which practices you are drawn to. Try the practices that you feel drawn to rather than the ones that feel burdensome. However, always also be aware that sometimes we do need to ponder the things that we have a strong internal resistance to. Ask yourself why you aren't drawn to certain exercises. Is that sense of disconnect something you might push into and see what's there? Is there an opportunity to grow in a new aspect of spirituality? Or is it just that it's a rainy day and a walk outside is unappealing?

As we discover what we already know about ourselves and about God, we can live into joy more fully with the choices we make each day.

RECORDING A DAILY EXAMEN
Days One to Ten

For each day, fill in what's bugging you and what's bringing you joy. Or, to put it another way: When did you feel far from God? When did you feel close to God?

You can have more than one answer. It's especially helpful to offer as many answers as come to mind for the joy question.

Here's space to fill in the first ten days (Day One questions are for each day).

DAY ONE

1. What's bugging you? _____

2. What's bringing you joy? _____

DAY TWO

1. _____

2. _____

DAY THREE

1. _____

2. _____

DAY FOUR

1. _____

2. _____

DAY FIVE

1. _____
2. _____

DAY SIX

1. _____
2. _____

DAY SEVEN

1. _____
2. _____

DAY EIGHT

1. _____
2. _____

DAY NINE

1. _____
2. _____

DAY TEN

1. _____
2. _____

> "There is something in every one of you that waits
> and listens for the sound of the genuine in yourself."
> HOWARD THURMAN

1

I HAD A BAD DAY

Paying Attention to the Beautiful Things

1. What's bugging you? _I burned the bacon and set off the smoke alarm._
2. What's bringing you joy? _Spotting a hummingbird on a hike._ _ _ _ _

I offered to cook the bacon so that Dan and I could start working. We were both working remotely from a warm and sunny spot in Palm Springs—a privilege we are grateful that our employers allowed. My parents had an unused timeshare week available, so we were housed at a nice resort.

The bacon cooked up nicely, but the smoke set off the kitchen alarm. We were on central time but I knew our neighbors were likely enjoying a Pacific time morning in their beds at five o'clock. So I grabbed the pan and set it outside the front door. We proceeded to open the windows and air the place out.

Then the doorbell rang. The two security officers asked if we were okay.

"Yes," I said with my pre-coffee eloquence. "Bacon."

"Bacon?" said the security officer.

"Yes, bacon," I repeated, and he left.

My pan was no longer smoking, so I leaned down to pick it up. Stuck. I pulled harder. It came off with a patch of welcome mat firmly attached to the bottom.

So my lovely day in Palm Springs started with scrubbing and scraping the welcome mat off the new-looking frying pan at the timeshare, and wondering whether we were going to be charged for the welcome mat's new indentation.

Some days are like this. Of course, they are not supposed to be the days away in a sunny location. *Where would the day go from here?* I wondered.

In this case, I had only goodness ahead. Sun. Time to walk. An early dinner. Watching the sun set on the balcony. But on a regular day with commuting and coworkers and pressures coming from every direction—well, the kitchen alarm could have easily taken me down.

For those of us in Western culture who live in privilege, it can be easy to lose sight of the big picture when we get a traffic ticket or lose a credit card. How can we get back on track when everyday mishaps distract us from our plans and goals for the day?

For me, paying attention to the tiny spots of beauty that are also at hand pulls me out of the "bad day" funk.

NOTICING SMALL THINGS

It's nice to think about those days that don't include a smoke alarm going off. The movie night with friends. The easy summer Saturday that ends with a glass of wine on the porch. On days like that, the first thing I want to write down is what brought me joy. Sometimes when I start writing, I notice more than one spot of joy and find myself writing a series of gratitudes. These are the days when it feels easy to connect with God and others. They are the days that seem to be filled with grace.

Gratitude leads to more gratitude. Writing down a moment of joy is leading me to notice more beauty.

My friend Christy Buckner Foster messaged on Facebook: "Post beautiful things, please." I eagerly clicked on the thread. There I saw the following:

- a happy cat and dog reunited after four months apart
- a GIF of Dolly Parton and Miss Piggy hugging
- a moonscape and a sunset
- a canoe on the water filled with flowers
- beaches
- happy babies
- horses
- more cats

We long for these moments of beauty after days filled with fake news and bad news but not nearly enough good news. And the Good News is that God is near. Stopping to savor these moments gives us the opportunity to stay connected with God all day long.

How can we bring more awareness of beauty into our lives?

Beauty can be found in the small things, in the details, like the tiny hummingbird Dan noticed on our hike later on the day-of-the-smoke-alarm.

> "Beauty is goodness made manifest to the senses."
> DALLAS WILLARD

Because he drew my attention to the one bird, then we were on the lookout. And we saw another and another. Each moment was one of connection between us and gratitude for this tiny, amazing creature of God's creation.

PRACTICE: MOMENTS OF BEAUTY

You can cultivate awareness of beauty within your own community by sharing moments of beauty with one another, just as my friend did. You can text images of beauty from your own life and talk about them with the people around you. Even when our posts don't go viral, we honor the gifts in our noticing.

I purchased a simple free app that allows me to add a quote to my own image and share that image on Instagram. In contrast to the extremes of either creating a false social media persona or ignoring real-world events, we can put a little joy out into the social media world and see what joy comes back our way.

CONNECTING WITH GOD IN THE GLORIOUS MOMENTS

I also regularly rotate the startup and lock screen pictures on my computer. There's a great one of my dad with our three kids. We went at Christmas and saw him in his men's chorus, so he's wearing his chorus vest. The kids said, "We came to see Grandpa's concert," which seemed like a fun reversal of the usual grandparent-grandchild dynamic. Dad is wearing his red chorus vest and everyone is laughing over something.

The tiny hummingbird Dan pointed out on the hill above Palm Springs is a new favorite.

Swiping past these pictures as I open the phone to pull up an app at the grocery store brings me back to these memories and gratitude for the moments of joy.

A hummingbird in Palm Springs

PRACTICE: PHOTOGRAPHIC EVIDENCE

Put a picture of a moment that represents a beautiful gift where you will see it often. When you see your picture again, offer a little word of thanks for that past happiness, and let that reminder open up a space of gratitude for you. Gratitude leads to more gratitude once we've gotten ourselves into a grateful mental space.

GET OUTSIDE

"You need to get outside. It's a beautiful day."

I heard this from my mom fairly often in the summer. I was an unathletic bookworm as a child and teenager. Actually, I'm still an unathletic bookworm.

19

My brother would go down the street to play basketball on a summer day and come home sweating and dripping to look for food. Mom would send him to the patio to drip or to the shower if he wanted to enter the house. He would repeat this process about four times a day.

I was happy reading a Nancy Drew mystery in our cool basement family room.

But somewhere along the way I did discover that Mom was right (as usual). Though you won't find me playing basketball, I have learned that I also love being outside. I love nature. I love walks. I'm learning to identify birds. I love gardening—for about an hour.

PRACTICE: A VISIO DIVINA WALK

I first learned about the idea of photography as a form of lectio divina (divine reading) called visio divina, or divine vision, from Christine Valters Paintner. Visio divina involves meditating on an image and asking God to speak to us in that. We can also "read" nature and nature can read (or speak) to us.

Take yourself on a walk with your phone and identify something that stirs you. Maybe it's lovely or interesting. Or maybe it's ugly. Watch your inner response. Both attraction and repulsion can be cues that there's something more. I like to take three to five of these images and sit with them. Sometimes I combine them in a photo collage. How do they speak to you?

Those gorgeous winter days in Palm Springs I was doing a bit of work and a bit of writing. Whenever I could, I sat outside on the porch or by the pool to work, and it brought me so much joy.

God is always reaching out to us, wooing us, especially through creation. Scripture invites us to picture God as a shepherd looking after each sheep in the flock. Ezekiel records the promises of the Shepherd: "I will tend them in a good pasture, and the mountain heights of Israel will be their grazing land. There they will lie down in good grazing land, and there they will feed in a rich pasture on the mountains of Israel" (Ezekiel 34:14). These images draw on God's invitations to us through nature.

Branches and Openings

A walk with God can also involve noticing what creates dissonance or a sense of ugliness. In these things, too, God can be drawing close and speaking to us. The Shepherd also promises: "I will rescue them from all the places where they were scattered on a day of clouds and darkness. . . . I will search for the lost and bring back the strays. I will bind up the injured and strengthen the weak" (Ezekiel 34:12, 16).

ESCAPING THE POLAR VORTEX

For me the opportunity use my parents' timeshare has been a mixed blessing. The booking process is incredibly tricky, and sometimes the original weeks my parents purchased have not been booked in time. Then there's an opportunity to redeem them back out of another system—which has a broad range of quality levels in terms of the properties included. So sometimes I end up feeling beaten down and frustrated by the system. It's just not well suited to my vacation needs and personality.

But it's still a free vacation! I am always grateful for that when I finally get there.

The stay in Palm Springs had its timeshare-related hitches as always, but it went better than usual, and it was a lovely property. And, best of all, the booking I set up a year ahead of time turned out to fall right in the midst of a polar vortex hitting Chicago. That alone was an event to celebrate. But there were the hiking trails, lots of fun, new restaurants, the art shows and galleries we visited, and more. So at the end of my time there I created an altar of gratitude as a way of offering thanks to God.

I took a prayerful walk around the timeshare looking for items that sparked my attention and seemed to call to me in some

PRACTICE: MAKING AN ALTAR

I learned about home–altar making from Anne Grizzle, who wrote a book called *Reminders of God*. An altar can be made indoors or outside. For example, you could pick up items on a walk, arrange them outside, use the altar for prayer and meditation, and then walk away from it as a way to reinforce the moment but not hold on to it. You can, of course, take a picture to preserve the memory and return to those moments of grace. Or you could gather items indoors on a table or shelf and keep them together as a reminder of grace when you pass by.

An altar of gratitude from Palm Springs

In my home I have a little prayer table near the chair where I sit to pray in the mornings, that holds objects of importance to me—crosses and a crucifix, part of an angel wing, a piece of cut granite, a Bible, and so on. I sometimes change this seasonally and add a purple cloth in Lent and Advent. This is a visual reminder of God's presence with me.

way—bark from a palm tree, seed pods, grasses—all reminding me of the beauty of those weeks. I noticed a golf ball in the parking lot. We didn't golf there, but golf courses were all around us in that location, so it seemed fitting. The whole experience was rather a mix of the natural beauty of mountains and hiking trails blended in with shopping malls and highly manicured properties with water features such as golf courses and the timeshare itself. I arranged it on a counter, took a picture, enjoyed looking at it for the next day, and then put the items back outside when I left.

2

I CAN'T BELIEVE I SAID THAT
Speaking Kindly to Ourselves

1. What's bugging you? *I said a rude thing to my friend.* _ _ _ _ _ _ _ _
2. What's bringing you joy? *I prayed and was reminded of God's* _ _ _ _
   deep love for me. _

I'll never forget that early morning in the college dorm. I was using the mirror in the hall to let my roommate sleep (see, I'm a nice person). A good friend stopped and asked me an innocuous question. But my running-on-not-enough-sleep brain couldn't surface an answer. So I said, "I hate you."

I was mortified that this response just came out of me. And she was one of my favorite people! To this day I can picture the hurt look in her eyes when I said it.

Fast-forward fifteen years and I still recall the time that I opened a gift of perfume from a dear friend. And these words came out: "Oh, I just saw this perfume in the store, tried it, and put it back on the shelf." Somehow, it didn't come out as "I can't believe you bought the very thing I was just looking at," but as, "I didn't want that." It was a free flow of thought from my brain out of my mouth without nuance. My friend's hurt response is clear in my mind: "I just gave you a gift. Why would you say that?"

Each of these events took place years ago, and yet I remember them so well. How do we recover when we say or do the wrong thing? How do we go about processing our own faults and failings?

HOW DO YOU TALK TO YOURSELF?

That was an unkind thing to say.

That was a dumb idea.

Why can't you be more patient?

How could you forget to do that?

Why are you so judgmental toward others?

These are some of things I say to myself—virtually on a daily basis. I never (okay, rarely) say such things to others. And certainly not multiple times a day. And yet I have an inner critic issuing a steady stream of these self-directed comments. I can get so busy beating myself up that it makes it difficult sometimes to differentiate between actions that are a part of living in a human body on this earth (forgetting my keys) and actions that cause harm to others (loudly expressing impatience for slow service at a restaurant).

> "Our courteous Lord does not want his creatures to lose hope even if they fail frequently and grievously. Our failure does not prevent him from loving us."
>
> JULIAN OF NORWICH

The first step is to realize that most of us can get stuck in this sort of negative cycle of self-judgment. We've been leasing an apartment in our brains to this inner critic for too many years. It could be a lifelong pattern. It could be a cycle that you learned as you internalized the voice of a parent or a teacher or a pastor early in your life. It could be that it is still reinforced by someone in your life who tells you negative things about yourself.

When you find yourself lapsing into negativity, what do you say to yourself? Something more negative?

Here's an idea: don't berate yourself more! For example, sometimes I find my mind wandering to negative thoughts about others. I notice this tendency, and I wonder why I can't meet each person with grace and love. Then I judge myself for being so judgmental! And none of that helps me to be better. So now I am a judgmental person who is also disappointed with herself.

Instead of beating myself up, I am learning to look to Jesus and offer myself grace—even in failure.

Show Yourself Grace

PRACTICE: MAKE A LIST

Marilyn McEntyre has a wonderful book by the title *Make a List*. She says "A list can be a valuable exercise in re-framing, which means seeing a situation in new terms." She suggests a great heading for a list would be "What doesn't matter as much as I thought." Other titles I've developed for lists include the following:

- Ways I Can Be Kind to Myself
- The Keys to Self-Kindness Are . . .
- Reasons God Wants Me to Be Kind to Myself
- What I Appreciate About Myself
- What I Need (but Rarely Give Myself)
- What I Don't Need

Make a free-form list. Let your mind wander and see what comes up!

WHAT DO YOU NEED?

The inner critic can be like a mean friend who tells you that you aren't good enough to be in their crowd, who makes you feel fat or clumsy or not cool. That voice needs to be either redirected to a more encouraging mode or simply shut down.

In her book *How to Be Yourself*, Ellen Hendriksen characterizes the inner critic as being like that terrible coach that attempts to motivate a child through harsh criticism and putdowns. This can result in the child simply giving up the sport. In contrast she describes a coach as one who encourages but who also offers guidance to help the child improve, "creating for ourselves a supportive environment in which we can try hard things."

Another way to address the inner critic might be to enlist the support of a friend or spouse to get another perspective. My colleague Al describes how he rebukes his wife's inner critic sometimes, saying things like "Be nice to my wife! Stop being mean to her." He says, "Some folks experience inner critics as self-bullying, and we need to have people we can go to who can defend us from the bullying." Hendriksen categorizes the examples here as "challenging" or arguing with the inner critic.

When we notice ourselves moving into a cycle of self-criticism, it also might be a signal of something deeper going on. We can pause and ask ourselves, *What do you need right now?* And then offer ourselves some words of comfort. We can remind ourselves that the voice of the critic is not to be trusted in these moments.

PRACTICE: WORDS OF COMFORT

As you become more aware of the inner critic, develop some mental patterns for your response when the negative thoughts plague you. Beware of the temptation to berate yourself more when you notice these thoughts surfacing! Instead, offer yourself words of compassion. You may even want to think of yourself as a small child who has fallen and skinned a knee. Have some ready phrases at hand for yourself.

Here in the "Make a List" format are some words of comfort that I have written on reminder cards for myself. I have phrased it as I would speak to a friend and then included meaningful Scripture references that affirm the truth behind these words.

Words of Comfort

God wants you to rest.
"The LORD . . . leads me beside quiet waters,
he refreshes my soul." Psalm 23:1-3

God will take care of you.
"Do not be anxious . . . look at the birds." Matthew 6:25-26 ESV

God is with you in this.
"The LORD shall be your rear guard." Isaiah 58:8 ESV

Be good to yourself.
"God is . . . the source of all comfort." 2 Corinthians 1:3 NLT

FREEDOM IN CONFESSION

Sometimes the inner critic has a good point! Consider whether you do hold responsibility for wrongdoing and whether there is anything you need to do to make it right. Do that. Or plan how to do that. When I baldly stated to my friend that I hated her, I needed to apologize. I did, and we were later able to laugh about it as a sign of sleep deprivation and stress.

I found myself confronted by the frequency of my critical thoughts toward others when I was editing *The Dangerous Act of Loving Your Neighbor.* In that book, Mark Labberton paints a vibrant picture of how many of us evaluate each other based on appearances and first impressions. It was another time that God spoke to me in the midst of my work. And it was an important realization. I want to look at people with the eyes of Christ rather than the eyes of a cranky editor.

When I notice myself lapsing into judging others, I can say things to myself like *Thank you, God, for allowing me to see this. Forgive me. Help me to continue to grow more in this area.* Then, hopefully, in that moment of confession, I can let it go.

Anne Lamott describes her process of becoming aware of how she was holding on to negative feelings toward another writer: "Then I turned in on myself. This is the great sin, the source of most madness and unease, so I took it to church, to the clinic. Hangdog, I confessed it in silence because it said to right there in the program, and because secrets keep us sick, cut off, in hiding, as if we were being stalked. I told the truth to God, that I have terrible thoughts. I couldn't promise to stop feeling so competitive and mean, but I mentioned that this grieved me."

One of the meaningful aspects of the liturgical worship tradition for me is having a time for confession each week— "in the program" as Lamott says. In many churches this portion is in a kneeling position—which I find to be a helpful engagement of the body with the spirit. We can pray this prayer on our own as well as in community as we name our sins before God and, as Lamott models, express our sorrow over them, asking for God's help to do better.

> "Self-transformation is always preceded by self-acceptance."
> DAVID BENNER

PRACTICE: THE LITURGY OF CONFESSION

This is a great prayer to memorize and pray as needed—
on your own or in community.

The Deacon or Celebrant says
Let us confess our sins against God and our neighbor.
Silence may be kept.

Minister and People
Most merciful God,
we confess that we have sinned against you
in thought, word, and deed,
by what we have done,
and by what we have left undone.
We have not loved you with our whole heart;
we have not loved our neighbors as ourselves.
We are truly sorry and we humbly repent.
For the sake of your Son Jesus Christ,
have mercy on us and forgive us;
that we may delight in your will,
and walk in your ways,
to the glory of your Name. Amen.

—*The Book of Common Prayer*

EXPERIENCING FORGIVENESS

Chapter one focused on God's gentle wooing through the gifts of
beauty in our days. But we can also picture Jesus more in the way of
Flannery O'Connor's character Hazel Mote: "a wild ragged figure

motioning him to turn around." In O'Connor's imaginative stories we meet a Jesus who pursues her bizarre and often unpleasant characters with a fierce relentlessness. When we feel lost, we can also picture Jesus as Hazel Mote did—in the background of our lives moving "from tree to tree." Jesus stays with us in our darkness and guides us into the light.

In the worship liturgy after the corporate time of confession, the priest speaks a word of absolution. The wording below is designed for daily prayer. It speaks well to our need to quiet our accusing minds. This prayer can be offered in settings where there is no priest present. If you need to hear these words today, read them aloud and know that in Christ there is grace for all of us.

> "Often the hardest person to forgive is yourself," said the mole to the boy.
> CHARLIE MACKESY

Merciful Lord,
grant to your faithful people pardon and peace,
that we may be cleansed from all our sins,
and serve you with a quiet mind;
through Jesus Christ our Lord. Amen.

3

BEYOND MY CONTROL
Creating a New Mental Playlist

1. What's bugging you? <u>My son is sick.</u> _ _ _ _ _ _ _ _ _ _ _ _

2. What's bringing you joy? <u>God spoke to me in the words of a lullaby.</u>

When my son, Spencer, was in his first weeks of life, he developed jaundice. The doctor instructed me to nurse him more often and to try to get him in the sunlight. But the jaundice continued. It became serious enough that the hospital sent over a contraption with a special phototherapy lamp to help increase his bilirubin levels.

The seat looked like an infant carrier with a light affixed over it, and he was to sit in it for periods of time all through the day and night. Of course, he didn't want to sit in it, and he cried. When he cried, every instinct in me demanded to pull him out of the seat. But if he didn't get better, I knew he would be admitted to the hospital so he could receive the light treatment around the clock. I didn't want that.

As a new mom, I was in a heightened hormonal state. Added to that was the distress and guilt over the situation (*It's my fault, I didn't feed him enough*). In addition to all that, his dad wasn't around a good bit of the time, and the emotional distance was increasing between us as well.

Those were nightmarish days and nights for me. And there was nothing I could do but wait and pray. Michael Card's recording of lullabies, *Sleep Sound in Jesus*, was my companion in the nights as it soothed both the baby and me: "Sleep sound in Jesus, sweetheart of my heart / The dark of the night will not keep us apart."

Even in the midst of it all, I was amazed and grateful that this healing light could be brought right into my home. As the jaundice faded, Spencer's sweet Aunt Angie comforted me saying that she thought he looked good with that very slight tinge of color on his face. The next doctor visit, with the terrible taking of blood by squeezing it from his little foot, showed that the bilirubin levels were down, so we escaped the threat of hospitalization.

CREATE A NEW MUSICAL LOOP

A double tape deck was a treasured device in my college years. With this off-the-shelf product one could create the ubiquitous mixtape. It took careful work to cue up the songs on each original tape, to start and stop the transfer to the blank tape at just the right counter point. To get in and out at the right moment. To avoid dead space or static. Or to repair the tape by winding it back in after it became a tangled mess inside the boom box.

The creation of these mixtapes was an art form, a way to archive just the right selection of music for studying or driving or a party.

Carrying a Lullaby

When a boyfriend or girl-friend passed mixtapes back and forth, it became a way of expressing deep truths and hidden messages that perhaps one did not yet have the words for. These days we have Spotify and other tools through which we can accomplish the same effect with much greater ease.

Favorite songs can bring me back to myself when I am in bad head space. And, as in the case of the lullabies I've described, in times of difficulty they can offer a refrain of comfort and joy. Music can bring us into the presence of God.

OUT OF CONTROL

We don't like to see each other suffer. I know that at some point I will sit with family members who will suffer much more than my infant son did under the phototherapy lamp. (I don't think he was in physical pain; he wanted to be held.) When it comes to health matters—whether our own health or the health of our loved ones—one of the hardest aspects is that so much is out of our control. We do our best to take the right actions by choosing the best medical facility and doctor and considering carefully the various options for treatment.

PRACTICE: A PLAYLIST

What are the songs that bring you joy? It could be the songs that are simply about joy and happiness. And it could be the songs that bring up memories of a moment, a concert, a parent, a place, and so on. They may also be the songs that resonate of the holy for you. Make yourself a playlist.

What are the songs that comfort you when you've had a bad day? The songs that reassure when something is really under your skin? Collect those as well.

I made Spotify playlists titled "What's Bringing You Joy?" and "What's Bugging You?" Here are some of the songs.

What's Bringing You Joy? Playlist	*What's Bugging You? Playlist*
"joy." For King & Country	"Rescue," Lauren Daigle
"Doxology," My Epic	"I Surrender All," Jadon Lavik
"10,000 Reasons," Matt Redman	"Psalm 91," Sons of Korah
"Great Is Thy Faithfulness," Chris Rice	"Silver and Gold," U2
"Turn Your Eyes Upon Jesus," Noah James & the Executives	"Have Your Way," Crossbeam
"Girl Shanty," Sons of the Never Wrong	"You Can Do This Hard Thing," Carrie Newcomer
"Girl on Fire," Alicia Keys	"Learn to Sit with Not Knowing," Carrie Newcomer
"On Top of the World," Imagine Dragons	"Sleep Sound in Jesus," Michael Card
"Holy, Holy, Holy," Sufjan Stevens	"Brave," Sara Bareilles
	"Be Kind to Yourself," Andrew Peterson

But we don't know when or if the pain will subside. We don't know if the treatment course or surgical procedure will cure us. Often, we don't even know why we are sick or hurt in the first place. For those with chronic illnesses, all of these issues are magnified.

Aging increases this loss of control with the slowing of the body and the mind. Author and friend Belinda Bauman describes what's bugging her as "the little indications that I don't recover physically from stuff as quickly as I used to when I was younger." Like it or not, we might not be as quick as we used to be. However, if we stay on a God-centered course, there are also ways that we grow as we age. Belinda continues, "On the other hand I recover emotionally much more quickly than I did when I was younger." There's the promise.

If we can learn to stay with our feelings, then we can develop the emotional resilience we long for in those out-of-control seasons and passages. And in the end that's the path to deeper joy. For me one way to stay with my pain and develop the emotional resilience Belinda is describing is to journal.

My mother has always seemed to imagine that my journals are a treasure trove that might one day be published. That's not the case—and I fully intend to destroy them before anyone else can evaluate them for publication! There's no *Diary of Anne Frank* buried in my box of old journals. What's there is more like an extended log of complaint, confusion, worry, and anger—interwoven with celebration and gratitude as well. My journal is the place I process with God. And sometimes it's the one place where I am the most honest about all my feelings.

PRACTICE: WRITE OUT YOUR PAIN

Journaling is an incredible tool for processing. I don't know how people survive without it.

Sometimes I do find a resistance in myself to writing about the really hard things. I don't want to dwell in it—I don't want to bring it back up. In some cases I don't want to have a record of it! But writing helps. Often in the process I discover more and more of what's really bothering me.

Try sitting yourself down and writing it out. Make it a brain dump, and keep going as long as you can. Challenge yourself to just write for fifteen minutes and see what comes. Then offer it to God.

COMFORT IN THE STORM

Another of the lullaby songs I was listening to in those difficult days with Spencer is called "Asleep in the Bow." In the refrain Michael Card marvels over how Jesus slept through a storm on the sea. One of the verses is:

Sweet Jesus, the storms in this life rage and howl,
so sometimes for little ones sleep's disallowed.
Raise up and speak now that storms may be gone
and make my waves calm now from darkness till dawn.

It's based on a passage from Matthew 8. This story offers us an image of giving up control from Jesus' perspective. The passage begins as Jesus gets into a fishing boat on the Sea of Galilee and his fisherman-disciples follow him.

> Suddenly a furious storm came up on the lake, so that the waves swept over the boat. But Jesus was sleeping. The disciples went and woke him, saying, "Lord, save us! We're going to drown!"
>
> He replied, "You of little faith, why are you so afraid?" Then he got up and rebuked the winds and the waves, and it was completely calm.
>
> The men were amazed and asked, "What kind of man is this? Even the winds and the waves obey him!" (Matthew 8:24-27)

I have found that this text is a good one to take up in dark and stormy days when I need to remember that Jesus is in the boat with me.

PRACTICE: MEDITATION, SLEEPING IN THE STORM

Put yourself in this boat. Where do you picture yourself? Can you rest like Jesus? Or are you distressed like the disciples?

What would it be like to sleep in a storm?

Now picture yourself as a tiny baby cradled by Jesus in that stormy boat. What is that like for you? Talk to Jesus about the feelings and desires this brings up in you. Allow Jesus to hold you in whatever way feels comfortable to you.

During those months of feeling so alone with a baby, I became deeply concerned and distressed about many things I could not control. The movie theater of my brain was full of dark scenarios, imagining potential future outcomes I could not know.

It was in this season that I reached out to a wise spiritual director, Marilyn Stewart.

I had long appreciated Marilyn from a distance, attending a seminar at a conference where she was teaching. I had some friends who had experienced Marilyn's wise counsel and spiritual direction. So I took a risk and asked if she would meet with me for spiritual direction, describing my marriage crisis. She graciously agreed to meet with me.

Marilyn was, at the time, sixty years old and was focused on offering retreats and spiritual direction to Christian leaders. Her countenance was always calm and reassuring. I immediately understood that she had seen and heard it all, having come alongside many people in crisis over the years. I had the sense that nothing I had to share would shock or surprise her. I also knew that I could not deceive her. I felt that she could see right through me. And yet I felt held and comforted by this aspect of her presence, not judged. Not ever dismissed or discounted. She could hold my feelings and needs but also see beyond them to what God might be offering me.

Marilyn encouraged me to pray just three words in these moments of negative and desperate thoughts, "Lord, have mercy." It was a simple and deeply helpful practice that I continue today when caught in a negative mental loop.

PRACTICE: THE JESUS PRAYER

A simple, beautiful prayer comes from the Eastern Orthodox tradition. It is found in an anonymous eighteenth-century Russian book called *The Way of the Pilgrim*.

It is in full, "Lord Jesus Christ, Son of God, have mercy on me, a sinner."

In the Orthodox tradition it is prayed repetitively in personal devotion or in worship. I find it a meaningful prayer to use when my mind is racing.

4

I SAW IT ON TWITTER
Knowing What to Let Go

1. What's bugging you? _My friend's political comment on social media._

2. What's bringing you joy? _Taking a break from looking at my phone this weekend._

Sitting in front of the TV, mindlessly scrolling through my phone, I came across a post from a childhood friend. I was happy to have reconnected with her on Facebook—to hear about her life and her family. But I'd recently been startled to see her political posts on issues that I also felt strongly about. I realized we were on opposite sides of many things. Things that connected with some of my core beliefs about kindness and human dignity.

As things on the political front heated up, her political posts seemed increasingly vitriolic to me. And they pained me. Yet again I wondered, *Should I unfriend her? Or perhaps just mute her?* Every time I would see her posts, these questions came up.

As I continued, post after post reminded me of the problems all around. Urgent problems. Issues I care about. Does it help if I comment or repost in agreement? What is my part in all of it?

Looking at Twitter that night only intensified these feelings of confusion and guilt. There people were talking about the news, and I realized I wasn't up to speed. I can learn a lot from reading the opinions of others. I like that about spending time on Twitter. It's an opportunity to follow and listen to diverse voices. I like that too. But there are so many big issues. Which ones should I take on? It's overwhelming.

> "Our lives begin to end the day we become silent about things that matter."
>
> DR. MARTIN LUTHER KING JR.

There are significant world issues that I do need to pay attention to. And the dialogue around these things is one aspect of the Twitter platform. But I find that I also need to consider how social media affects me after a long day of work. Now and then I become aware that I need to stop and reflect on where and how I am engaging.

I find the words of the Serenity Prayer define for me the sort of discernment that is needed to know where to add my voice to the noise and where to let go. It reminds me that I am not in control.

PRACTICE: THE SERENITY PRAYER

This prayer has long been a centerpiece of twelve-step groups and has been a lifeline for many. It is attributed to Reinhold Niebuhr and thought to have been written in 1932, although there is some controversy and doubt over the authorship. Nevertheless, the prayer is a gift and a source of grace for those moments when we need to acknowledge that we are not in control. It can offer clarity in those instances when we wonder what conversations we are or are not called to step into.

> God grant me the Serenity
> to **accept** the things I cannot change,
> **Courage** to change the things I can,
> and the **Wisdom** to know the difference.

I SHOULD NOT HAVE READ MY EMAIL

I was at a Saturday night concert with both Carrie Newcomer and Over the Rhine—two of my longtime favorites. Dan and I went out for a great dinner at a Latin fusion restaurant that was new to us, and we got to the concert venue early. While waiting for the start, I was messing around on my phone a little. I thought of something that I had intended to do for work. It was just a little thing: following up about an item to purchase for the office. So I opened my email and pasted a link in a message that I would send on Monday morning.

While my inbox was open, I saw an email response regarding something I'd been worrying over earlier in the day. I thought the response would be a reassurance that things were taken care of. In this way I justified opening it. Unfortunately, the message there was decidedly not a reassurance.

As a result, during that remarkable concert I fell into a negative head loop about that email. The bad news of the email was compounded by the fact that I had broken my own long-established pattern of email use. I knew that I was miserable due to my own actions, which then led to some negative self-talk.

I have set some ground rules for myself in regard to how I use email.

1. Shut it down at least a couple of hours before bed. Several days a week, I like to keep it shut from the time I return home from work.

2. Don't reopen email until I get back to work!

3. Keep it completely shut down at a minimum during my sabbath practice from 5 p.m. Saturday to 5 p.m. Sunday.

When I stick to my ground rules, I find them incredibly helpful.

In *Sacred Rhythms*, Ruth Barton describes her daily morning rhythm with attention to how she engages technology. She keeps a two-hour morning routine in quiet at a slow pace while getting ready with no technological stimulation at hand. She includes time for silence and time for Scripture reading. Then Ruth proceeds with "getting dressed and making other preparations for the day and sometimes even a short walk, but doing so quietly and prayerfully rather than allowing other kinds of stimulation." To think that getting dressed could be a part of a God-centered morning routine has opened up some possibilities for me as I have thought about how to make space for God in my own busy day. However, I've gained the most benefit from setting careful boundaries around the use of technology.

I generally try to stop work at a certain point in the early evening. Then I try to keep the practice of not opening my email from the time I go to bed until I get to work. Flipping through messages that I don't have time to answer before I depart in the morning just loads up my mind with all there is to do. Then I am getting stressed or writing emails in my head while I drive when I could be relaxing a bit. Or—worse yet—is when I try to write a quick response before I've had coffee. For me this inevitably results in an ineffective communication.

This rhythm of shutting down work and focusing on family and inward reflection is somewhat like the monastic practice of a "Great Silence" overnight. Those of us who live with family and friends probably wouldn't find a literal silence to be desirable, but there's a pattern and rhythm to the monastic wisdom that we can embrace. Ruth Barton writes, "Unplugging from certain aspects of technology can be a symbolic act of releasing the work of this day to God and being fully present to the gifts of eventide: a shared meal, conversation with family and friends, contributions made to life at home, leisure and rest." It's been helpful to me set aside email and social media in order to offer myself a gentle way to close one day and then begin the next.

PRACTICE: EMAIL MANAGEMENT

Think about your relationship with email in the morning and throughout the day and evening. Does email—or the content of specific messages—show up on your list of what's bugging you? What do you notice about your stress levels as you engage email? Are there any changes or adjustments you would like to make to how you manage email?

SOCIAL MEDIA PAIN POINTS

With the way that Facebook shows us our own history, we can find ourselves surprised to be faced with memories of broken or lost relationships, for example. My friend Melody put it this way: "Facebook has a way of showing you memories of the biggest mistakes of your life. . . . When hopes and dreams are destroyed, it changes things. It changes you." But then she went on to encourage those who are feeling these regrets that we can we can find freedom from the past.

At other times social media spaces become places of trauma. The election of Donald Trump in the fall of 2016 was a moment of intense pain for many people, but especially for people of color. Sheila Wise Rowe helped me understand what the aftermath of this election was like for an African American woman through her insightful book *Healing Racial Trauma.* She writes, "Each day insults and assaults were coming from the White House." And then she continues, narrating her observation of her own online engagement,

PRACTICE: SOCIAL MEDIA FAST AND RESET

There are many ways that we find freedom from the ever-present pull of social media—drawing us to comparison or worry or judgment of others. For some, Lent is a good opportunity to go offline for forty days to gain more time to read and pray. For others there might be a weekly sabbath day from social media. Still others might fast for a season of focused work on a project to regain energy and margin, to allow the mind to focus.

The advantage of taking a break of any length is to give an opportunity for you to check in with yourself and see how you feel with and without social media in your life. There's no one answer for everyone, but it's worth looking deeply at the question of whether your social media use is bringing you joy. And then, to get the full benefit of the fast, reset how you engage social media.

Time for a Reset

"The signs of unprocessed trauma were evident in my responses which ranged from silence to oversharing, survivor guilt to being triggered by the latest news cycle." Observing in herself these signs of racial trauma was the beginning of a post-election healing journey for Sheila. She was eventually able to attend a listening prayer workshop that provided a breakthrough for her in healing.

Our ever-increasing levels of engagement with social media may actually be lowering our level of happiness. A December 2018 article published in the *Journal of Social and Clinical Psychology* cites a new study with students at University of Pennsylvania. Senior and coauthor of the paper Jordyn Young wrote, "What we found overall is that if you use less social media, you are actually less depressed and less lonely, meaning that the decreased social media use is what causes that qualitative shift in your well-being." It would seem that perhaps less time on social media leads to greater joy.

In an episode of the podcast *Hurry Slowly*, Cal Newport said, "Twitter is an anxiety machine." He also talked about the trend of people taking a break from social media and cautioned that taking a break from social media is like saying you are taking a break from heroin! It's unusual not to simply walk right back into the same social media patterns. For that reason, he says that a break or fast needs to be combined with a simplifying or "declutter" that offers some new ways of engaging social media—such as not putting certain apps on your phone.

SOCIAL MEDIA REDEMPTION

I was getting close to blocking or removing my childhood friend in order to avoid her political posts. And then came a post that surprised me. It read something like this:

> I realize that I have been frequently and strongly been posting my political views. I realize that I have dear friends who may disagree with me. I realize that there's room for us to disagree on these matters. I may not have everything right. So if I have hurt or offended you with anything I have posted, I apologize.

I did not see that coming. If I had shut her down—even just by hiding her posts—I would never have seen this beautiful and redemptive post. I would not have had the opportunity to be reminded that God's love is wide and encompasses all of us. Sometimes people do change! Ironically enough, on that day it was Facebook that reminded me of that.

RECORDING A DAILY EXAMEN
Days Eleven to Twenty

How's it going? Take a midpoint assessment look through your list for the first ten days.

What do you notice about what's bugging you?

What do you notice about what's bringing you joy?

Here's space to fill in the next ten days.

DAY ELEVEN

1. _____

2. _____

DAY TWELVE

1. _____

2. _____

DAY THIRTEEN

1. _____

2. _____

DAY FOURTEEN

1. _____

2. _____

DAY FIFTEEN

1. _____
2. _____

DAY SIXTEEN

1. _____
2. _____

DAY SEVENTEEN

1. _____
2. _____

DAY EIGHTEEN

1. _____
2. _____

DAY NINETEEN

1. _____
2. _____

DAY TWENTY

1. _____
2. _____

> "Life moves pretty fast. If you don't stop and look
> around once in a while, you could miss it."
> FERRIS BUELLER

5

RINGING IN MY EARS
The God Who Sees Me

1. What's bugging you?   _I am hurt by the comments and actions of others and am doubting myself._

2. What's bringing you joy? _Through Scripture and spiritual direction, God is showing me my true self._

Early in my professional life, I was coming back from lunch with a group of coworkers, and we began talking about a male colleague and how he related to women. I commented that I liked working with him. The response came back, "He doesn't get along with strong women." The implication, of course, was that I was not a strong woman, and that was why I got along well with this male colleague. It planted a nasty little seed of self-doubt in me—the sort that sprouts up like a dandelion that's hard to get out of the ground and, when left in place, can spread.

I wrestled with my relationship with this colleague in light of this comment in the coming days—questioning my actions, wondering if my continued good relationship with him meant that I was not being strong. Wondering why these women—there were two involved—would say such a hurtful thing. I worked up the nerve to talk with one of the women further at a later date but got a brush-off.

As the dandelion seeds spread into new ground, I found myself slipping into negative mental cycles again and again. I wondered, *Am I not a strong woman? Do I need to change my relationship with my male colleague because I am failing in some way?*

GOD HEARS AND SEES

Scripture is one place I turn to when I am wounded. Although I know I am separated by thousands of years from the people and events of Scripture, I can find myself in these stories. More than that, God's Spirit can speak to me in a moment of need through the sacred Word. Hagar's story in Genesis 16 has been one such place of comfort for me.

In this text Hagar, a slave, is given by Sarai, her mistress, to Sarai's husband, Abram, because Sarai herself could not become pregnant. Hagar is now pregnant. Sarai feels that Hagar now despises her, so she complains to her husband about Hagar. Abram says, "Do with her whatever you think best" (v. 6). And the text tells us that Sarai "mistreated Hagar."

Hagar has no place of safety. She's been betrayed by both her mistress and the father of her child. So she runs away.

We meet Hagar alone in the desert. An angel finds her near a spring, and the angel begins to talk with her, offering a vision of many descendants who will follow from her son, but also describing how her son will be a person who is at odds with those around him. The angel says the son will be named Ishmael, which means, "God hears."

Hagar responds by offering a name for the Lord: "'You are the God who sees me,' for she said, 'I have now seen the One who sees me.'"

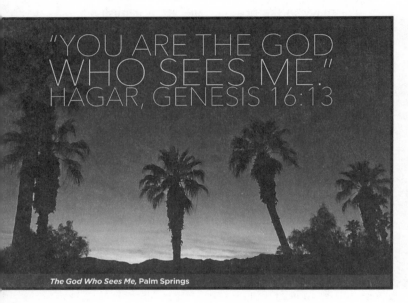

"YOU ARE THE GOD WHO SEES ME." HAGAR, GENESIS 16:13

The God Who Sees Me, Palm Springs

When I have been treated unjustly or felt cast out in some sense by others, I have found it helpful to place myself in this scene, finding myself in the presence of an angel of God in a pleasant oasis in the midst of the desert. I have never heard the whole story of my future as Hagar did, but I am reminded that God sees and knows me intimately.

My friends Gayle, Karen, and Mary Jean led a retreat in which they worked with this passage with an approach called "Thought Rhyming." They first learned this form of meditation from the book *Joyful Journey,* which points out that Hebrew poetry rhymes thoughts rather than sounds. That concept led the *Joyful Journey* authors to explore ways to weave our thoughts and God's thoughts together: "We know that as we become intimate with someone, we begin to finish each other's sentences and thoughts. . . . This is exactly what can happen between us and God too." *Joyful Journey* presents a pattern of praying that helps us to connect our thoughts with God's thoughts. To model this pattern, beginning with Hagar's experience, Gayle imagines God seeing her, writing it out in this way:

> I see you on your patio as the day dawns. I see you basking in the sweet peace of the morning. I see you embracing these moments of silence. I hear your calming breaths. I hear your body's aches and pains too. I hear your gratitude for small things. I understand your desire to know what is next. I understand the ways in which fear dapples your day. I understand that you want to find your way home—to joy and peace. Gayle, I am glad to be with you and hold your weakness tenderly. I can refresh your body. I can offer you more peace, more love. I can meet you at the Communion table this evening.

It's a process that fosters a deeper and closer connection with God and a sense of how God speaks to us.

PRACTICE: THOUGHT RHYMING

Follow the pattern below to write out your own thought rhyme picturing God speaking to you in the following four ways. Begin where you are right now. Write down what you hear from God.

1. *I can see you.* Hagar says, "You are the God who sees me" (Genesis 16:13). *Describe where you are and what you are feeling right now.*

2. *I can hear you.* Of the son she is carrying, the angel says, "You shall name him Ishmael, for the LORD has heard of your misery" (Genesis 16:11). *Continue writing to yourself in God's voice. What is God hearing in your inner thoughts? Are you judging yourself? Is your breathing shallow or deep? Are you excited? Afraid?*

3. *I can understand how hard this is for you.* When we look at Hagar's situation we are likely to feel compassion for her. However, as noted in *Joyful Journey*, "Often we deny ourselves permission to receive comfort for the seemingly small moments of pain. We minimize our apparently minor trials, compared to the perceived bigger

Asking God for help in the last step of the thought-rhyming process is where I get hooked or stuck and often need guidance. While I don't believe in a God of easy answers, in reality my prayers have often focused on how God might resolve things in life according to my agenda and timing. I was about to learn more about how to discern and embrace God's true promises to me.

changes of others. We do this to ourselves and to others. God, however, sees, hears, knows and understands why a particular issue is so big for us." *Write out words of compassion and understanding from God to you.*

4. ***I am glad to be with you.*** In Hagar's story we see God take the initiative to approach her in the form of an angel. Whether what's bothering us is from an external cause or a result of our own error, God is never repelled from us. God always wants to come near and offer healing and presence. *What do you sense God offering you?*

5. ***I can do something for you.*** The angel of the Lord offers a promise to Hagar: "I will increase your descendants so much that they will be too numerous to count" (Genesis 16:10). God also tells Hagar to return to her mistress—a very hard thing. God always offers presence. And there are other good gifts around us as well. In Gayle's example God offers her physical rest and the gift of the Communion table. *How will God be with you and help you?*

GOD SPEAKS

Spencer's father left me when our son was nine months old. Many words were spoken between us. Words that planted seeds of doubt about how I saw the whole history of our relationship and marriage. And about how I saw myself and my own value.

For a period of time I had some hope and desire that he might return and the marriage could be redeemed. I wanted to seek God in a deeper way and understand what God wanted from me in all of this. Truth be told, I was hoping that God would tell me my future as the angel did with Hagar.

I made arrangements to make a four-day overnight retreat at St. Procopius Abbey in Lisle, Illinois. Marilyn Stewart agreed to meet with me each day and offer spiritual direction and guidance. St. Procopius is a Benedictine abbey. Participants are invited to pray and sing or chant with the monks to mark the liturgical hours at five times in each day. This created a structure for my day. There is also a monk designated to host meals, chatting with the guests and visitors. This is all part of the Benedictine vision for offering hospitality.

I was well cared for and had points of contact with people so that the solitude did not close in on me. Nevertheless, it was a dark and difficult time. Lots of tears. Lots of wrestling. With Marilyn's help, I was able to process through a lot of things—including my expectations of God.

I came to understand that God was not going to force my husband to repent and return to the marriage. God designed us to be people who choose freely. I also began to understand that God had invitations for my husband, as well as for me. But the only choices I could control were my own.

As we came to the end of the retreat days, Marilyn said to me, "There should be a promise. I believe God wants to offer you something from Scripture."

I'd been reading the book of Isaiah and engaging the practice of lectio divina. This form of Scripture meditation takes us out of our heads and into the presence of the Spirit so that we can hear God's voice speaking specifically to us from the sacred text.

When I came to 43:10, I was stopped short by the words "my servant whom I have chosen." I knew deep in my soul that those words were God's words for me.

"You are my witnesses," declares the LORD,
    "and my servant whom I have chosen,
so that you may know and believe me
    and understand that I am he.
Before me no god was formed,
    nor will there be one after me."

In my muddled thinking I believed that my witness and even my work in Christian publishing was compromised by my husband's choices. But through this text God affirmed a calling for me.

PRACTICE: LECTIO DIVINA

The process of reading Scripture in the lectio divina style is quite simple. Pick a passage—not more than a chapter of the Bible, perhaps less. (Some possible key texts for reflection are at the end of the chapter.) Then read through the whole passage three times. Read it aloud at least one of the times. You could also listen to it on a Scripture-reading app. Be alert for a word or brief phrase that stirs you. It might even bug or provoke you. This is not a time of study or analysis of the text but of simply focusing on a word. Ask God about your word or words. What is the message of these words for you today? Offer gratitude for what you hear. The final step of this process is simply quiet contemplation in God's presence.

Marilyn affirmed this when I shared it with her. Then when she prayed for me, she had a vision which was "The road is long, but the path is broad." They were words pointing to the difficulty ahead—not unlike the ominous words about Ishmael that Hagar heard—but there was also a hope and lightness in the promise of a broad path.

REMINDERS OF LOVE

I made myself a scrapbook in this season of separation. In it I placed the notes and cards and letters from friends and family. These notes were reminders of their love. There were words of wisdom, poems, and Scripture verses. All of them gave me hope and deep comfort. These sorts of tangible reminders of love carried me through some dark days. These kind notes helped me to remember to be kind to myself. I added pages with key Scripture verses that reminded me of God's love for me and pointed the way toward hope. One passage that was very moving to me at the time was "The LORD is near to the brokenhearted, / and saves the crushed in spirit" (Psalm 34:18 NRSV). I began "illuminating" these texts with art as a way of meditation.

Marilyn Stewart's husband, Doug, wrote in a retreat guide about the ways that we experience God drawing near in all of our emotions: "God is with us, in spite of appearances to the contrary, and our own faults and feelings of desolation and fear. God knows our thoughts and our situation and wants to bring life-giving words into our lives, that we might be renewed in energy, joy, and hope, and live as those who are 'waiting on the Lord.'"

These days on my desk at home I have a handwritten note that my grandfather wrote me some thirty years ago on the Bunch Company Real Estate stationery. My grandfather rarely wrote to me, and the note seemed reflective of him and his values. It said simply, "Work hard. Save your money." But to me it also says that he was thinking about me and cared about my life.

The LORD Is Near: "The LORD is near to the broken-hearted and saves the crushed in spirit" (Psalm 34:18 ESV). Red and white tissue on black background, 1999

When a group gathered over lunch at the office to talk about spiritual practices that nurture us during the workday, a key item that emerged was reminders of who we are as God's children. They are things that bring us back to ourselves when work or life gets a little stressful. Things like the following:

- a favorite quote hung on the wall
- a hand-drawn picture of Jesus from a child
- a simple wooden cross to pick up and hold
- a pen given by a mentor

Scripture passages can work like this for me. There are Scripture passages that I come back to in seasons of doubt or pain or confusion. They are the passages that help me to know that I am uniquely loved by God. Rereading them reminds me of the times I have felt that God's Word is speaking directly to me.

The image of God as a shepherd protecting the sheep and leading them to goodness in Psalm 23 is a powerful one. I created a collage that helps me to think of God guiding me like a shepherd when I am overwhelmed with the work in front of me.

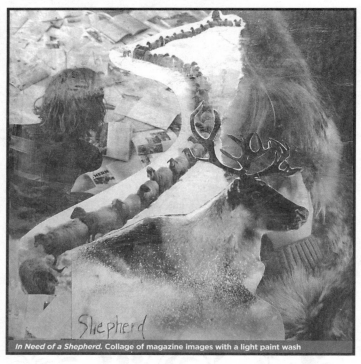

In Need of a Shepherd. Collage of magazine images with a light paint wash

PRACTICE: REMINDER CARDS

Linda Richardson, an Anglican priest and spiritual director, has a delightful pattern of passing out lovely 3 x 5 inch cards with a Scripture text and image to accompany a sermon or a retreat she is leading. These cards are wonderful resources for prayer and meditation. They also serve as reminders for where we have been with God and for what we have learned. You can create your own reminder cards.

Select about five meaningful Scripture verses or God messages—words that God is speaking you. For example, Hagar's words: "You are the God who sees me." Or this: "Do not be anxious about your life, what you will eat or what you will drink, nor about your body, what you will put on. . . . Look at the birds of the air: they neither sow nor reap nor gather into barns, and yet your heavenly Father feeds them" (Matthew 6:25-26 ESV). Write each verse on one side of a small card, 2 x 3 inches or 3 x 5 inches.

On the reverse write a brief phrase or message to yourself with empathy. Express your thoughts as you would speak to a friend. For example, "It's okay for you to feel this way." Try using "seeing" language, imagining a friend who knows and loves you no matter what.

If you wish, add images using collage (you can cut pictures from a magazine) or your own illustration to create something that encourages you.

Here are some verses that are a reminder of God's love for us and that point the way to self-kindness.

The LORD is my shepherd, I lack nothing.
    He makes me lie down in green pastures,
he leads me beside quiet waters,
    he refreshes my soul.
He guides me along the right paths
    for his name's sake.
Even though I walk
    through the darkest valley,
I will fear no evil,
    for you are with me;
your rod and your staff,
    they comfort me.
You prepare a table before me
    in the presence of my enemies.
You anoint my head with oil;
    my cup overflows.
Surely your goodness and love will follow me
    all the days of my life,
and I will dwell in the house of the LORD
    forever. (Psalm 23)

For you created my inmost being;
    you knit me together in my mother's womb.
I praise you because I am fearfully and wonderfully made;
    your works are wonderful,
    I know that full well. (Psalm 139:13-14)

The LORD longs to be gracious to you;
    therefore he will rise up to show you compassion.
For the LORD is a God of justice.
    Blessed are all who wait for him! (Isaiah 30:18)

Then your light shall break forth like the dawn,
    and your healing shall spring up quickly;
your vindicator shall go before you,
    the glory of the LORD shall be your rear guard.
        (Isaiah 58:8 NRSV)

His father saw him and was filled with compassion for him.
        (Luke 15:20)

Jesus saw them following and asked, "What do you want?"
        (John 1:38)

6

WHEN LIFE'S ON HOLD
Establishing Self-Care Practices

1. What's bugging you? _I am grieving my marriage._____

2. What's bringing you joy? _I am remembering to care for my own___
   _basic needs._____

During the months of marital separation, I was alternately sad, angry, hopeful, panicked, lonely, and numb. We were going to counseling, and I was holding out some hope that he would want to reinvest in our marriage. In some ways that made it all the more confusing. I was waiting for him and trying to understand what God was asking of me—and what I even wanted for myself. My retreat had helped to ground me in God's love, but I still ran through the stages of grief on a daily basis.

I was back at work, which provided a strong support network and enjoyable tasks to occupy my days as an editor. I was also still nursing, a new mom trying to find my way of doing the working mom thing. My milk supply was starting to suffer from the stress of work demands and the separation, so that was another thing to worry about. How could I live with this stress, this uncertainty?

I remember taking the rare opportunity to treat myself to an outing at a lovely mall in those early months of motherhood. I wandered about with Spencer content in his stroller, and yet I felt so aimless. Nothing was interesting to me. I was numb.

A STATE OF GRIEF

The seasons when what's bugging us is a pretty major life stressor—moving, job loss, divorce, illness—we may find ourselves in a state of grief similar to that of grieving a death, creating a sense of numbness to everything else. Or we may find ourselves in a place of extreme anxiety. We walk around like little hermit crabs, staying deep inside our hard shells but longing to find a soothing place to lay our heads and rest. But nothing feels comfortable or reliable or safe.

Seeking Comfort

Times of intense stress are when we need to have familiar tools at hand to sustain us. It's hard to learn new things when your mind is either racing or blank. In her Enneagram training courses I have often heard author

> "Have courage for the great sorrows of life and patience for the small ones; and when you have laboriously accomplished your daily task, go to sleep in peace."
>
> VICTOR HUGO

Suzanne Stabile say, "Everyone needs a therapist and a spiritual director. Get one now so that you are ready when you need them. 'Cause you will."

"What do you do when something is bugging you?" I asked my co-worker Joaquim. He told me that he takes a nap or gets a good night of sleep. Then he starts making an action plan. His response—that he rests before he starts tackling a problem—surprised me. He's one of the most productive people I know. But his plan is wise. It points to the basic ways we need to care for ourselves in order to be ready to tackle the problems we face.

In *The Good and Beautiful God* the first soul training exercise James Bryan Smith assigns to the reader is sleep! He writes: "Sleep is an act of surrender. It is a declaration of trust. It is admitting that we are not God (who never sleeps) and that is good news. We cannot make ourselves sleep, but we can create the conditions necessary for sleep." Jim says that many readers have commented to him about how much they appreciate starting their spiritual journey with sleep!

Here are some of my self-care essentials:

- Long walks
- Maintaining connections to family and close friends
- Regular worship
- Scripture reading
- A spiritual director
- A counselor
- Sleep and rest
- Eating well

PAY ATTENTION TO YOURSELF

When I was young, the dinner table was often a place of laughter—sometimes to the point of tears. At one mealtime I recall what happened when my brother—maybe seven years old at the time—spilled food on himself several times. Our father looked at him and said in his deep father voice, "Pay attention to yourself, son." That made us laugh, and it became an often-repeated phrase in our house.

Though my brother was the one called out at the table that day, I have realized that I am also guilty of this. In the process of deepening my acts of self-kindness, I am learning to pay more attention to myself—especially my physical self. Where am I holding stress or pain in my body? Getting in touch with that helps me to unfold what's bugging me. And it helps me to heal.

I have found incorporating a very modest yoga practice—no headstands for me—into my life has helped me to be more aware of my body, to work off nervous or angry energy, to attend to places of pain and tension, or simply to relax. I found a great YouTube teacher whose approach gives me the space I need to bring my own faith to the mat. So when I do a bit of yoga, I connect with God and reflect on the movement of God within me. I am grateful for my body and my Creator.

However, if I'm going to be completely honest, I will confess that I initially found the breathing exercises in yoga somewhat annoying. *I'm here to stretch and get a little exercise; I can breathe on my own time,* I would think. But in time I've become more aware of how shallow my breathing is. I can feel myself start to hold my breath! It's good for me to remind myself to breathe deeply each day.

PRACTICE: BODY SCAN

Take a moment to check in with your body head to toe. Close your eyes and pay attention to your scalp, your face, your neck, shoulders, arms, fingers, torso, your thighs, calves, feet, and toes. Where do you feel pain? Let it go. Tiredness? Invite God to fill you up. Notice your breathing. What's it like? Take a few deep breaths and let them out. This is a practice you can pick up several times a day just to check in with yourself and how you are feeling.

WORSHIP

The complexity of the season of marital separation meant that it was best for me to leave our church. A season of grief is not really the best time to be looking around for a church home. It took me about five years to really find myself settled in a church community again.

Although my faith was rooted in the American Baptist Church, for some time I had been drawn to the liturgical tradition. During my Baptist seminary years some of my friends and I had started sneaking into to Catholic and Anglican services.

Marilyn's spiritual direction for me in this season was that I embrace liturgy. Liturgy doesn't demand a lot of you—though it does offer an opportunity for bodily engagement and assent as you stand, sit, kneel, and respond verbally. It can become a place of comfort and routine in a space of distress. Marilyn said that the weekly Eucharist would be healing for me. So I started attending an Anglican church with a lovely, warm spirit. I didn't try to engage with people. I would just go and follow the liturgy, and it began to take root in me.

In a season when we feel that life is on hold, we may find that the words don't readily come. *The Book of Common Prayer* is full of beautiful prayers that have been used for centuries and are, right now, being prayed all around the world. Praying these prayers offers a spiritual connection to the communion of saints past and present.

Here are a few passages from *The Book of Common Prayer,* beginning with morning prayer.

O God, the King eternal, whose light divides the day from the night and turns the shadow of death into the morning: Drive far from us all wrong desires, incline our hearts to keep your law, and guide our feet into the way of peace; that, having done your will with cheerfulness during the day, we may, when evening comes, rejoice to give you thanks; through Jesus Christ our Lord. Amen.

In her writing Tish Warren has drawn my attention to this bed-time prayer for the liturgical hour of Compline.

Keep watch, dear Lord, with those who work, or watch, or weep this night, and give your angels charge over those who sleep. Tend the sick, Lord Christ; give rest to the weary, bless the dying, soothe the suffering, pity the afflicted, shield the joyous; and all for your love's sake. Amen.

Particularly in a season when sleep is difficult, this is a helpful prayer.

"The Prayer for the Oppressed" is a powerful prayer to pray when you have no words for the pain and suffering of this world.

Look with pity, O heavenly Father, upon the people in this land who live with injustice, terror, disease, and death as their constant companions. Have mercy upon us. Help us to eliminate our cruelty to these our neighbors. Strengthen those who spend their lives establishing equal protection of the law and equal opportunities for all. And grant that every one of us may enjoy a fair portion of the riches of this land; through Jesus Christ our Lord. Amen.

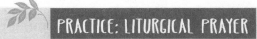

The psalms were also a great comfort to me in my season of grief. The ancient words of prayer echoed both my sorrow and my rage. I felt abandoned, ashamed, bereft. The psalms gave me words for what I was experiencing when I had no words to pray. The psalms give us permission to bring all of ourselves to God. Psalm 71 particularly resonated.

In you, LORD, I have taken refuge;
>   let me never be put to shame.
In your righteousness, rescue me and deliver me;
>   turn your ear to me and save me.
Be my rock of refuge,
>   to which I can always go;
give the command to save me,
>   for you are my rock and my fortress. (Psalm 71:1-3)

PRACTICE: PRAYING THE PSALMS

For the past few years the team of editors I work with has gathered each Monday morning to read a psalm aloud together. It's a wonderful discipline to pray the psalms one by one, as the psalms have many moods. The psalmists remind us that we can bring all of our emotions to God. You might want to try speaking the words aloud as you pray to incorporate the sense of hearing. Here are some psalms for different spiritual and emotional needs. Let the words of psalms give you freedom to offer your own pain and joy to God.

Anger: Psalm 55; 140
Sadness: Psalm 13; 119:81-82
Anxiety: Psalm 27; 37
Grief: Psalm 43; 55; 77
Joy: Psalm 34; 103
Hate: Psalm 18:16-19

THE JOY AND THE PAIN

In the letters he wrote from prison while awaiting his execution, Dietrich Bonhoeffer wrote about how we experience grief after the loss of a person we were very close to. I believe that what he writes here can be true of many types of loss: "The more beautiful and full the remembrances, the more difficult the separation. But gratitude transforms the torment of memory into silent joy. One bears what was lovely in the past not as a thorn but as a precious gift deep within, a hidden treasure of which one can always be certain." For me the treasure I held from my marriage was my son.

This deep joy Bonhoeffer describes is the fruit of leaning into whole-body practices that support us as we allow ourselves to feel grief and pain. It is the fruit of seeking gratitude, of seeking God in the midst of pain. As we learn to care for ourselves and lean into the things that deepen us, we find new pathways to joy.

7

IT WASN'T SUPPOSED TO RAIN TODAY

Discovering What's Underneath

1. What's bugging you? *My flight was canceled.* _____

2. What's bringing you joy? *Making a collage put me in touch with* ___
   my feelings. _____

I planned only one brief trip this summer—to meet my parents and
my brother and his family in the Poconos for a long weekend. It had
been a hot July in Chicago, and I was anticipating sitting by the cool
lake on a rare visit. Dan kindly drove me to work so I could head
directly to the airport at five o'clock. It was a stormy summer day,
and my flight was delayed after I arrived. Just an hour. The airport
was about as full of waiting passengers as I had ever seen, over-
flowing onto the floors in front of the gates. And the flight was delayed another hour. Then the gate changed. Then another delay. After
four hours of delays I headed to another gate where a plane was at

the ready. Just as the boarding was about to begin, the flight was canceled. No more flights were available for the whole weekend. I got a refund and took a Lyft back home at 10:30 p.m. Defeated.

Weather disappoints. Friends back out on plans. Flights are canceled. Sometimes these changes leave us at loose ends. And our minds spiral with thoughts of what was supposed to happen but is not happening.

I asked some friends what they do in these instances. My friend Christy Pauley wisely said that if it's not something within her control, she tries to "forgive or accept and then busy myself with a hobby or something productive." She continues, "That will improve my mood and keep me from dwelling on it." Then she confessed that sometimes distraction turns into a Netflix binge. It's good to have friends who keep it real!

In these situations we need to sit for a moment and get in touch with our own feelings of frustration or disappointment. However, there may be other times when the best course is not necessarily to try to sit and meditate but to get up and do something else: to play a board game with a child, go for a walk or a run, try a new recipe.

And yet it's also easy to choose Netflix. Or to go shopping. Or to spend hours on social media. Or fill the time by playing a computer or online game. As we reflect on some of our familiar patterns, we need to give ourselves a bit of grace, but we also know the truth is that these distractions don't necessarily cultivate the deeper joy we are seeking.

Holy distractions draw us away from what's bugging us and into God's presence. These might not all be things we think of as "spiritual." They could include woodworking or gardening or knitting or cooking a new dish or playing an instrument. I am thinking of the activities that help us to relax and take our minds off what's bugging us.

Defining what is or isn't helpful distraction might be different for different ones of us. I like to practice a sabbath rest from work and chores on Sundays. Sometimes I garden on Sunday. I try to keep that light and fun in a way that feels creative and connects me to the earth. However, gardening can easily be overwhelming when I work too long, or the weeds are too many, or I get into a "getting things done" mode rather than a restful frame of mind. It's something I try to monitor within myself as I think about how to spend my Sundays.

PRACTICE: HOW DO YOU DISTRACT YOURSELF?

Make two lists. First, list some of the negative ways you typically distract yourself when you are sad, angry, or frustrated. Put it on a piece of paper rather than in a journal, and tear it up if you want to. Then offer it all to God.

Then return to your list of joys for the past ten days. List one or more things you'd like to take up as holy distractions next time you are really bothered, and add other ideas as you feel prompted.

Give yourself space for a guilt-free process. The goal here is to identify the things that do and don't bring us joy. The holy distractions are not intended to be new tasks for your already-too-long list or to make everything about productivity.

PRAYING WHEN IT'S HARD TO FOCUS

So how can we approach prayer when we are frustrated, distracted, disappointed, or simply unfocused?

Centering prayer, which has been taught by Father Thomas Keating, has been a helpful practice for millions. In this practice you sit in silence for a timed period and focus on a word and/or an image. There's a great app called "Centering Prayer" that offers a quick tutorial on the practice and a timer with a centering gong sound.

Centering prayer is an antidote to quiet our wild and unruly minds. Teresa of Àvila wrote, "The harder you try not to think of anything, the more aroused your mind will become and you will think even more." In teaching centering prayer Villanova professor Martin Laird refers to the early church father Evagrius, who discerned "the difference between the mere presence of a thought and something within us (he called it a passion) that seized the thought and whipped it up into a frothy obsessive commentary." Laird continues, "These obsessive patterns within us generate anxiety, suffering, and the sense of restless isolation from God and others." Centering prayer offers us a way to still our minds and focus on God.

However, the truth is that centering prayer is tough for me. I make the attempt sometimes because I know it's good for me to get quiet. I practiced centering prayer regularly at Marilyn Stewart's recommendation during my sabbatical. But here's what happened recently when I attempted six minutes of centering prayer.

Things I Thought About During Centering Prayer

- My neck hurts
- Cat is cozy on my lap
- Mary's birthday party
- Summer vacation
- Do I have the right prayer word?
- Fire in the fireplace
- Neck still hurts
- My hair is still wet from my shower
- Writing a poem about what I thought about doing centering prayer
- Facebook
- Six minutes is a long time
- The fire in the fireplace went out

"Doodling prayer" is another form of prayer that I have found helpful. It's a way of praying while writing or drawing. I find it to be a helpful way to focus given the busy monkeys that are always at play in my brain. The idea here is not so much to write out a prayer list as to draw and doodle about what we want to communicate to God. I can list the names of the people I want to pray for. I can write out what I'm thankful for or what I am longing for. And as I write and pray, I can color and doodle around the words that are the focus of my prayer.

ART AS A TEACHER

The act of creating something takes me out of myself and helps me center my thoughts on God. It also reveals layers of what's really going on inside—worries, hopes, regrets, dreams.

PRACTICE: DOODLING PRAYER

I learned doodling prayer from Sybil MacBeth. You can find resources, including Lenten and Advent templates at her prayingincolor.com. A simple way to start is to draw out a wavy line and then add leaves large enough for you to write a name. Fill in the leaves with the names of the people you are praying for. Then doodle around the leaves adding color and berries.

A template for doodling your prayers

I have never considered myself an artist because I find drawing difficult. But I love to make collages from magazine pictures. Noticing the images I gravitate to helps me unearth what's inside when I'm all stirred up. The process of concentrating on the images, the physicality of cutting and pasting, all of those things help to pull me out of my head. Then I pray and journal my thoughts about what I see before me. It can be surprising what comes up.

PRACTICE: COLLAGE

Pick four or five pictures from magazines to fit on a piece of 5 x 8 inch cardstock. Try to find a mix of people or animals with nature as well as material objects or architecture. Focus on images without words to open up your mind as to what meaning you might attach to the images. As you choose, notice both what you are drawn to and what repels you. Both kinds of images might be important for you to work with. I first learned this process from Margaret Campbell, former Renovaré board chair, and she recommends including a living being in at least one of the pictures. Glue the images down with a glue stick. Then sit in quiet and ask the Spirit to speak to you through these images. Journal about what you discover.

I began the collage *Creatures* with the gripping image of suburban deer looking into a porch window in the middle of winter. It

Creatures, magazine images on cardboard

was a way for me of grappling with my own frustration with the long Chicago winters. I added to this the leaping whale—an animal that fascinates me; the parakeet—a bright, exotic indoor bird; the standard poodle, which reminds me of my father-in-law's charming farm poodle, Jacques; and this young heifer—a sign of spring birth on the farm. All of it combined put me in mind of the fact that I, too, am a creature under the care of the Creator. Putting it all together is a sort of sequence of association, allowing each image to stir me to consider another. Then I prayerfully make the connections from one to the next.

Another way I've experienced the power of art is through a class with Sheri Abel. Sheri is a spiritual director and a French professor at Wheaton College who has developed a monthly class experience that intentionally draws together spirituality and intuitive art around the process she first learned at The Open Studio Project in Evanston, Illinois. It involves setting an intention, doing a "brain dump" journal session, exploring art making in a wide-open right-brain process, and then journaling about the experience.

As Sheri describes it, the art making is about

- play, which is restorative
- following your impulses and curiosity, being willing to let what you've started creating to morph into something else
- stepping into creating without an agenda, without trying to control what the artwork looks like
- being in a place of vulnerability, showing up with the intention of openness
- trusting and surrendering to the flow of the creative process—how God has designed our body, soul, and mind to work

Sheri writes: "It's not about skill. The art that you make is a souvenir of the process and what came through your work. It's about journeying with the Lord as we learn to relax and go with the flow of the creative process."

I find the intuitive process both freeing and relaxing. It helps me to explore what I am feeling and to discover what's underneath.

One evening in Sheri's class the way the art making played out for me is that I started out painting layers of color on a large piece of brown paper that I had taped to the wall. I then sponged over it all with sparkly gold paint. It felt fun and free. And the gold paint unified the colors. But then I looked at it and felt stuck in the same way of painting I'd followed in previous sessions. So I took down the sheet of paper and cut it into long strips. Then I began weaving the pieces together. It was a long process but felt satisfying.

After a while I realized that I couldn't finish weaving in the time available. I gave the art a turn, and then the strips were dangling. I liked this as it felt at once woven in and free. Then I saw some small mirrored circles among the objects that Sheri had provided for our use. I interspersed some of them throughout the woven sections.

When I came to the reflective writing portion of the experience, it struck me that the mirrors provided a signal to see myself reflected in the art. I thought about how the art became more beautiful to me (in a relative way—it's not fine art!) when I cut it apart. This seemed to me like an experience of suffering that can cause me to feel that I am being taken apart, and then how God can remake me as a result.

The weaving aspect caused me to reflect that while it is sometimes tricky to be woven in close to people and still feel that we have freedom, this is the experience we have in life with God. The more tightly we are woven in with God, the freer we are.

God showed me all of this through the experience of prayerfully playing with paint and paper for ninety minutes in the company of other faithful seekers. I had no idea when I arrived on a regular weekday evening where I would be traveling with God.

8

I CAN'T BELIEVE HE DID THAT

Forgiving Others

1. What's bugging you? _I am angry about what he's done._

2. What's bringing you joy? _Letting go of my anger._

First, I shredded up cards and letters.

I progressed to taking glasses, mugs, and other small objects outside to smash on the sidewalk or patio in the backyard—out of the sight of others.

Then I looked at the built-in brick fireplace on the patio that we had used to grill meals, and to enjoy relaxing in Adirondack chairs on a summer evening. It was a feature of the house I had loved at first sight. I thought about a building a fire. I could burn some things from the marriage that felt significant; it could be a path to releasing some of the pain. I thought it would also help me make concrete for myself that this terrible thing was really happening. He was filing for divorce. The marriage was over.

So, as in the other instances of destruction, I chose a time when I was alone and selected some symbolic items—gifts he'd given me, some pictures, items I'd saved from the wedding—and built a small fire.

It helped a little. Another step in a long journey I never wanted to take.

When I shredded, smashed, and burned things, I was not thinking of it as a spiritual practice. But years later I was reminded of this step in my journey as I worked with Beth Slevcove on *Broken Hallelujahs*.

PRACTICE: SMASHING THINGS

Out of the sight of children who might find this shocking or scary, Beth Slevcove recommends smashing dishes as a way to grieve, which will, as she put it, "allow my mind and muscles to work out pent-up anger from some hurt I've received." Then she says that after sweeping up the pieces, she sometimes makes them into a mosaic as a way of creating something beautiful out of her grief. Or, alternately, she just throws all the pieces away.

Experiencing and releasing anger is another way of accepting ourselves. When we acknowledge our inner pain and frustration, when we voice our most difficult questions to God, when we feel all of our feelings, then we open ourselves up to the opportunity to heal. We aren't dwelling on the negative. We are opening our darkest thoughts to the Light. We examine them in a safe space, knowing that the warm light of God's love will be the beginning of our healing and transformation.

Mary Mrozowski developed the concept of welcoming prayer based on the teachings of Jean-Pierre de Caussade in the eighteenth century along with the contemporary teaching of Thomas Keating. The prayer allows us to begin to get in touch with all that we are feeling and then to release our feelings to the transforming light of God's love. In welcoming all that we are feeling, we are being real with ourselves and with God rather than shoving down the feelings that seem less mature or less spiritual or simply less desirable. Welcoming prayer smooths the way for deeper levels of self-acceptance and eventual forgiveness. Thomas Keating has written a prayer that provides guidance through the process.

PRACTICE: WELCOMING PRAYER

In a relaxed posture, breathe deeply, and pray through the following words.

The Welcoming Prayer
Welcome, welcome, welcome.
I welcome everything that comes to me today
because I know it's for my healing.
I welcome all thoughts, feelings, emotions, persons,
situations, and conditions.
I let go of my desire for power and control.
I let go of my desire for affection, esteem,
approval, and pleasure.
I let go of my desire for survival and security.
I let go of my desire to change any situation,
condition, person or myself.
I open to the love and presence of God and
God's action within. Amen.

—Father Thomas Keating

THE GAZE OF LOVE
During these years of healing, one of the most loving, faithful interpreters of God's view of me was Marilyn Stewart. She could see my

faults and help me name them. But the conversations with her were so full of tenderness and love that it was never difficult to bear the hard things. I knew she believed in me—often beyond what I believed for myself. She could and would draw out of me more and more of who God intended me to be. Her gaze, though penetrating, was always filled with love. This is what God's love is like.

In *The Gift of Being Yourself* David Benner writes: "Genuine self-knowledge begins by looking at God and noticing how God is looking at us. Grounding our knowing of our self in God's knowing of us anchors us in reality. It also anchors us in God." God's gaze is full of love.

The gaze of God's love builds us up. It calls us to let go of the things that harm us and others so that we can flourish in the light of grace. The gaze of love allows us to become our true selves.

In Luke 7 we read of Jesus' encounter with a widow as he enters the town of Nain with a crowd of followers. The widow's dead son is being carried out, and there are crowds with her. It sounds like an overwhelming mass of people converging.

When Jesus saw the widow we are told that he "had compassion on her." The text continues:

> Then he came up and touched the bier, and the bearers stood still. And he said, "Young man, I say to you, arise." And the dead man sat up and began to speak, and Jesus gave him to his mother. Fear seized them all, and they glorified God, saying, "A great prophet has arisen among us!" and "God has visited his people!" And this report about him spread through the whole of Judea and all the surrounding country. (Luke 7:14-17 ESV)

In a contemporary oil painting of the scene, a coffin is being carried out and the widow looks out at the viewer of the painting. As we meet her gaze, we see

Widow of Nain by Egbert Modderman

the pain on the widow's face. We don't see Jesus in this image, but we can imagine him gazing back toward her. The painter is inviting us to enter the scene and meditate on it.

PRACTICE: MEDITATION, MEETING JESUS' GAZE

Picture yourself as one of the people in this scene. You might choose to place yourself as an onlooker, a pallbearer, the widow, or as the dead son.

What do you see, hear, feel?

Look at Jesus. What is it like to make eye contact with him?

What does Jesus want from you?

What is Jesus offering you?

Now step back from this encounter with Jesus and look to God. What is your sense of how God sees you?

Is there any difference in how you picture Jesus' gaze and God's gaze? If so, why do you think this is?

Sit with all that has come to you. Ask God reveal the gaze of love to you now and in the coming days and weeks.

DEEPENING FORGIVENESS

I knew I was supposed to forgive my ex-husband. Early on, Marilyn helped me understand that there was a difference between being at a point where I could forgive and being at a point where I could reconcile. The latter never happened. Yet over time I thought I had forgiven him. I was past breaking and shredding the things that were a part of the marriage. I was past that heavy feeling of hate. I think I had reached a point that might be best described as numbness toward him. As the years passed, I felt free to date and to think of a future with someone else.

Eventually, I met Dan and his daughters, Maggie and Mary. The joy of that new relationship brought up new feelings of grace in me toward my ex. This change in me was further advanced by Dan's expression of happiness for me and for Spencer, who at five years old was talking frequently about how much he liked being with Dan, Mary, and Maggie. For the first time I understood that if my ex did not really want to reinvest in the marriage, then the best thing for me was for him to move on. He had set me free. And with the help of God and a caring community, I was able to seek love again.

I moved from a vague lack of hate for my ex to actually wishing him well. It had taken four years. It felt great. It was the journey of knowing who I am as a daughter of God that got me there. I discovered these words in *The Message* version of Scripture painted a glorious picture of this remarkable transition from hate back into the experience of love.

But me he caught—reached all the way
    from sky to sea; he pulled me out
Of that ocean of hate, that enemy chaos,
    the void in which I was drowning.
They hit me when I was down,
    but GOD stuck by me.
He stood me up on a wide-open field;
    I stood there saved—surprised to be loved!
    (Psalm 18:16-19 *The Message*)

RECORDING A DAILY EXAMEN
Days Twenty-One to Thirty

How's it going? Pause to look through your list now that twenty days have passed.

What do you notice about what's bugging you?

What do you notice about what's bringing you joy?

Here's space to fill in the last ten days.

DAY TWENTY-ONE

1. _____

2. _____

DAY TWENTY-TWO

1. _____

2. _____

DAY TWENTY-THREE

1. _____

2. _____

DAY TWENTY-FOUR

1. _____

2. _____

DAY TWENTY-FIVE

1. _____

2. _____

DAY TWENTY-SIX

1. _____
2. _____

DAY TWENTY-SEVEN

1. _____
2. _____

DAY TWENTY-EIGHT

1. _____
2. _____

DAY TWENTY-NINE

1. _____
2. _____

DAY THIRTY

1. _____
2. _____

> "Praying is no easy matter. It demands a relationship
> in which you allow someone other than yourself to
> enter into the very center of your person, to see there
> what you would rather leave in the darkness, and to
> touch there what you would rather leave untouched."
>
> HENRI NOUWEN

9

I CRACKED UNDER THE PRESSURE
Taking One Thing at a Time

1. What's bugging you? _I overscheduled my day and ended it by yelling at my kids._

2. What's bringing you joy? _Finding ways to slow down the pace of my day._

After Dan and I had been married for about eight years, we decided to use our accumulated miles and take a family trip to Europe. So we headed to Ireland with three teenagers.

It was midmorning when we arrived in Dublin on a glorious summer day. I get a huge adrenalin surge at the opportunity to see a new place, so I was ready for sightseeing. Everyone else wanted a meal that in my view took much too long. I managed to get everyone to over to Trinity College for a tour, but they were dragging from the overnight flight. While the oldest, Mary, was still interested in sightseeing, when I looked around for the other two kids, I found them lying down on the lovely quad grass hoping for a nap. So our day in

Dublin wrapped up early as we went to the hotel in the outlying country-side near Wicklow. The hotel was a beautiful place, and although day one had not gone according to my plan, we had a restful night.

I had done my research and had the route all mapped out for the next day. While I'm not normally a planner, I do enjoy planning vacations because it allows me to dream a bit about what it will be like. I love reading about the place we are going to and imagining all the things we could do. I pack into the itinerary as much as possible—and then more, just in case something doesn't work out or we have extra time or we change our minds about what we want to do. The anticipation is part of the fun for me.

If we got going early, I thought, then we could stop for lunch and see a castle ruins on the way to our bed and breakfast on the coast in the town of Dingle. A number of the guidebooks mentioned that the drive was on windy, difficult roads (like everything in Ireland, I learned) and could take longer than the GPS indicated. So I was worried about the driving time.

We had two hotel rooms, and Maggie and Mary did not wake up on time. We banged on the door and called, but still they did not wake up. Finally we got them roused, dressed, and out of the hotel. It was such a lovely hotel. No one wanted to leave.

We stopped in town for breakfast at a little bakery. I just wanted to

> *The most important aspects of our lives cannot be rushed. We cannot love, think, eat, laugh, or pray in a hurry. . . . When we are in a hurry—which comes from overextension—we find ourselves unable to live with awareness and kindness.*
>
> JAMES BRYAN SMITH

grab a scone and go. My need to get on the road was getting stronger and stronger. It took a long time to get our scones. Another thirty minutes lost.

I was in a foul mood.

By the time we got to the town with the castle ruins, everyone wanted lunch. So we went to a pub. Again, of course, it was slow. (I wasn't accounting for the fact that Irish restaurants are, of course, not focused on speed in the way of American restaurants.) Finally, we were able to go see the castle. We raced through it so that we could get on the road. The guidebooks said that you didn't want to be on the road to Dingle after dark. But the kids didn't seem interested in the castle anyway. Another fail for me. Too late I realized that I shouldn't have planned that stop. I just made everyone miserable.

The drive time was just as the GPS said it would be, and we got there in good time. But my mood remained foul. The kids were slow and didn't want to get up and go to dinner.

At the end of the day as we sat in a local pub listening to music, I ended up yelling at Mary in such a loud manner that we were asked to leave the pub. My desire to fit everything in and capture the moments in Ireland left us all with a bad day to remember—the result of overscheduling and the overtiredness that comes with international travel, coupled with some of my persistent flaws such as impatience and judgmentalism.

JUST BREATHE

A practice that has carried me through many difficult, overscheduled days—though, unfortunately, it did not come to mind in

Ireland—is breath prayer. I first learned it from Adele Calhoun in her extraordinary *Spiritual Disciplines Handbook.* Through meditation or prayer or simply spiritual habit, we pray a short line with each breath in and a corresponding line expressing our desire with each breath out. The Jesus Prayer (chapter three) could be incorporated into breath prayer, for example. Short lines from Scripture can also become our breath prayer.

My friend Wai Chin tells me that when the brain is in stress mode, our ability to rationalize with ourselves is shut down. For this reason, it's helpful to plan ahead with simple go-to spiritual practices that we learn to turn to whenever the stress hits.

PRACTICE: BREATH PRAYER

One of the approaches to breath prayer that Adele Calhoun suggests is to state a name of God with an inward breath and then a character quality to match it on the breath out. She offers these examples.[1]

Breathe in "Abba," breathe out "I belong to you."
Breathe in "Healer," breathe out "speak the word and I shall be healed."
Breathe in "Shepherd," breathe out "bring home my lost son."
Breathe in "Lord," breathe out "here I am."

Choose a prayer and come back to it throughout your day as a reminder that God is near.

CHOOSING THE SLOW LANE

In order to ease into the workday, I try to set up my drive to work to be as relaxing as I can make it.

For eighteen years my day began by getting my son to a sitter and then eventually to school. During his elementary years, we had the gift of a school bus that stopped next to our house, but I still had to get him out the door. During his high school years, I was much more stressed about getting him there on time than he ever seemed to be. And we cut it close fairly often. So I'd move on from the school feeling the adrenaline letdown of having achieved the first deadline of the day.

Now, when I drive by his schools, I miss the drop-offs, and especially the pickups. When my son was young, my wise author and friend Jan Johnson encouraged me not to miss the times in the car with him. And she was right. Those were often my most productive and satisfying opportunities to talk with him.

To improve my drives, I have applied the concept of intentionally choosing the slow lane. I learned this from Linda Richardson. She offers this spiritual counsel for choosing both a grocery store line and a lane of traffic. It's a way to practice going more slowly in a small daily way.

In suburban Chicago we maximize our drive time by changing lanes frequently if things slow down. But I have found a more restful way to deal with driving is—often, not always—to pick a lane and stay in it! If I just wait out the person making the left turn, I only lose seconds to minutes. And I save myself the stress of trying to whip around them. It's a spiritual practice for me.

Another practice I follow is to diligently avoid the temptation to look at email or social media while driving. When I'm driving, my phone is only for GPS, podcasts, music, and audio books. Of course, we know this is the proper safety practice, but it could be that some of us slip in this area sometimes. I can choose not to multitask at stoplights.

Typically, I have some form of entertainment playing while I am driving. But sometimes I find my mind wandering. Or I just need quiet. The car can become a sacred space. I have found it helpful in periods of my life to play the same music every time I get into the car. The repetition becomes restful.

Worlds Opening Before Me

The most radical change of all is to stop driving. Some of us live in areas where that is possible. My colleague Jon starting biking to the train—rather than making the long drive from the city to the suburbs—so that he could get to work in a more relaxing way. A further benefit is that he gets some work done on the way into the office. And he also has built in time to exercise by biking to the train. He's finding it to be a much more satisfying way to handle his commute.

PRACTICE: IMPROVE YOUR DRIVE TIME

When and how do you spend most of your driving time? What would you like to do to find more joy or connection with God in your car time?

As the day goes along, the overwhelming number of tasks that are simultaneously demanding my attention can add stress to my day. As an editor I always feel the tension between the completed manuscripts with the nervous authors waiting for my first reading, the revised manuscripts awaiting my second, third, or fourth reading—with both an author and a managing editor waiting for the book to move on to copyediting—and the rest of the things that need to be done to make a book. Should I instead work on the details that are needed to get ready for the next catalog list—titles, endorsements, cover copy? Manuscript boxes and covers literally pile up at my door. I am an editor who is also a manager. That means other people are waiting for me to respond so they can do their work. And there are financial reports to read, meetings to plan and attend, contracts to approve, and much more.

Sometimes I find my breathing pattern may start to shorten. I may even notice that I am holding my breath. I have to remind myself to breathe. I pick up my small smooth holding cross and invite God to enter my day.

RETURNING TO SELF-KINDNESS

I've rethought that day in Ireland more than once now. I have so many regrets.

Brené Brown says that regret is a function of empathy: "I believe that what we regret most are our failures of courage, whether it's the courage to be kinder, to show up, to say how we feel, to set boundaries, to be good to ourselves. For that reason, regret can be the birthplace of empathy." So there's the comfort of knowing that regret means that I am growing as a person. And the opportunity to practice self-kindness again.

10

THINGS I DON'T WANT TO DO
Gratitude Flip

1. What's bugging you? _I need to get an emissions test on my car._

2. What's bringing you joy? _Connecting with God in the midst of the boring stuff._

It was the Saturday before Memorial Day. I needed to get an emissions test on my car. I'd left it to nearly the last minute, since the emissions center was closed on Sunday and Monday. On Saturday morning at nine I made my way over there, thinking I had plenty of time to get it done. A couple miles away, the road backed up. This seemed odd on a Saturday morning in the suburbs. After fifteen minutes or so, I was able to turn a corner and got a better view. This line of cars was headed in the same direction I was. A look at my GPS showed a long, red line the rest of the way there. It was all traffic extending far out of the emissions center, down the road, backed up for at least a mile. I bailed.

I decided I would just get up early on Tuesday morning—my last day to get the test—and get in the line before it opened. I'd be late to work, but it had to be a better option than this.

I spent the weekend in a low-grade dread over what I'd find there on Tuesday and how much work I'd need to make up. But mainly, of course, I was kicking myself for not getting there sooner.

Here are a few of the items that I procrastinate about.

I don't want to

- call the dentist to make an appointment
- pay the bills
- do my expense report at work
- get the oil in the car changed
- fill out the FAFSA documents

It's some of the most mundane stuff of life that drains me. Of course, I know at a certain level there's a privilege that lies behind each of these—that I can afford medical care, that I have a job, a car, a child in college, and more. I can talk to myself about privilege. But I need to do it in a way that doesn't evoke guilt.

THE RELATIONAL STUFF

But there's more stuff that I don't want to do. Some of it gets more serious because it leads me into relational conflict, transparency, and vulnerability.

> *Time spent avoiding and stressing about graduate school assignment: 14 days, 24/7. Time spent doing actual assignment: 2 hours."*
> LORI NEFF,
> FACEBOOK POST

PRACTICE: TURN IT INTO GRATITUDE

My friend Jacci Turner shared a practice she learned from her spiritual director. The idea was to "stop ruminating over things by being fully present and thankful for what I am doing." When doing the dishes, Jacci would say to herself, "Thank you for these dishes I get to wash because I can feed my family." She found it helpful when she was in the midst of a cycle of negative thoughts.

I Love Doing Dishes. **Photo of a sculpture at Palm Springs Art Museum with collage elements added**

This is an effective way to slowly change over those negative mental states, perhaps especially the activities that lead to the "Why am I stuck doing this chore?" internal conversation.

I don't want to

- respond to the email asking me to do just one more thing
- tell my coworker how upset I am
- explain to a friend why my feelings are hurt
- apologize for being impatient

Why do these particular things bother me? Is it that I've allowed my personal or professional boundaries to be violated? Is it that I just prefer to avoid the conflict? Is it that I am worried that my feelings are out of proportion? Is it that I am embarrassed?

In the novel *Barefoot* Sharon Garlough Brown narrates a conversation between a married couple that opens up the idea that there might be something more to the things that are bothering us—especially when we move from the mundane to the relational realm.

John asks Charissa about some counsel she has received from one of her professors: "What did you say you learned from Dr. Allen about paying attention to stuff that bugged you?"

Charissa recalls, "Learn to linger with what provokes you."

This leads John to share his discomfort with his relationship with their pastor—who was first Charissa's pastor from her childhood years until now. John has felt like an outsider in the relationship and in the church. It's a difficult subject for him to raise knowing how bonded she and her family are with the pastor and the church. However, talking about it creates a space for greater openness and trust in their marriage.

This novel offers us a helpful model for pausing with the things that are bugging us and considering them with a little more care.

PRACTICE: LINGER WITH WHAT'S BUGGING YOU

What's underneath the things that nag at your mind? Is there a pattern?

Take a look through your listing of what's bugging you.

Ask God what you can learn from the thoughts that plague you. What is your part in these situations? One thing I've discovered from recording what's bugging me is that when everyone around me seems to be wrong—I am probably the one who has the problem!

Remember to speak kindly to yourself about whatever you discover.

MOMENTS THROUGH THE DAY

One of my most common conversations in spiritual direction with Marilyn would begin with me saying something like, "It would be easy for me to be more spiritually grounded if I could be in charge of my own schedule each day. I look around at people I know who have grown children or who don't go into an office. Sure, they work hard, but they can also schedule a retreat day."

Marilyn's response was that instead of focusing on the major times of rest—like retreat—I could create small daily habits that would remind me to connect with God.

Thanks to my husband's determination, we were able to establish a pattern in which each person would get their dishes into the dishwasher. But no one cleans out the sink. I walk in and find pieces of food sitting there. This bugs me. So Marilyn encouraged me to make the times when I am cleaning out the sink a time to pray specifically for my family.

Yardwork is a chore that is fun for me for about twenty minutes. Then I get bored. To make it less draining, I listen to podcasts, often ones on spiritual themes. This keeps me from getting into an irritated, bored brain loop, and instead I'm engaged and learning. I might even have something interesting to say about the podcast when I go inside.

 ## PRACTICE: GOD IN THE MUNDANE

Consider the things that bug you on a regular basis—perhaps tasks that are part of your routine. Are there any that you can turn into times for prayer or gratitude or to which you can add an element of fun by playing music or listening to a podcast?

11

SECOND-GUESSING MYSELF
The Wisdom of the Enneagram

1. What's bugging you? *I'm second-guessing my decision to move.* _ _ _ _

2. What's bringing you joy? *The Enneagram gives me a window into* _ _
   understanding why I do what I do. _ _ _ _ _ _ _ _ _ _ _ _ _ _ _ _ _

Dan and I bought an 1897 Victorian house and held a wedding ceremony right there. Our three children were our attendants, and our friends and family gathered on folding chairs. Then we moved in.

The house was in a great location—walking distance to the city center and steps from a commuter train just twenty minutes from Chicago's Loop. We did a lot of work on it over the next thirteen years, beginning with transforming the faded pink paint exterior to a lively gingerbread pattern and ending with a brand-new, top-of-the-line upstairs bathroom. We were very proud of the house, but it had worn us down. With Spencer, the youngest, headed to college, we were ready for something newer, requiring a little less work. And I was longing for a little more natural beauty around the house—a bit farther away from the Starbucks whose cups sometimes were left at the sides of our yard by passersby. So we put our house on the market.

I was so sure of the house that I convinced Dan we should go ahead and buy a house before we sold our current house. We could afford a couple months of overlap. The market was stronger than it had been since the recession. So as we were putting the house on the market, we put down a deposit on our next house.

Perhaps you can guess what happened: our lovely old Victorian didn't sell. Many potential buyers required a master bathroom. Others wanted a finished basement. One thought our faithful cast iron radiators looked dangerous. And so on. We owned two houses for one month, two months, and as summer was coming to a close, we began to fear that we had lost our window to sell.

Just as we found ourselves in the midst of this situation, my husband's job role started to shift around in surprising ways—and all this was taking place while we were paying for college education for two children.

Life was feeling out of control. And I was second-, third-, and fourth-guessing my choices! I knew I had driven this sequence of events due to both my own desire for a different home and some vague inner sense of calling. Now we were in a precarious financial situation. I was riddled with guilt and self-doubt.

How could I live with myself?

LEARNING FROM THE ENNEAGRAM

The Enneagram approach to self-understanding has been a huge help to me in offering myself a little bit of kindness when something's bugging me. Knowing what space or number I occupy on the Enneagram helps me to understand what pulls me down. It reveals what I am like when I am most my true self—operating out of the most positive attributes of my number. It also reveals what I look like when I am living in my false self—with exaggerated traits of the most negative aspects of my number or the number I relate to (see the arrows in the diagram below).

Because I am an Enneagram Four, often called "The Romantic," I crave beauty. That can lead to good things—like noticing small gifts from God throughout the day or making the spaces I inhabit more attractive. But being a Four means I can also move to a place of dissatisfaction, restlessness, and envy. "The grass is always greener" is a truism for a Four. These downsides may very well have led me to try to force a move to happen when it was not necessary and financially risky.

PRACTICE: KNOW YOUR ENNEAGRAM NUMBER

Did the above paragraphs sound like a foreign language? Have you taken the time to learn about the Enneagram and find your Enneagram number? If not, pick up a book that will help you to get a handle on your number. *The Road Back to You*, a book I edited (full disclosure!), is a favorite of mine. For some people finding their number is quick and intuitive, and for others it can take some time. But it's an extremely fruitful spiritual exercise.

I first learned the Enneagram from Alice Fryling. On one of my early dates with Dan, I showed him the notebook I had received in her class, and we talked about how the Enneagram reflects both our best and worst traits. We mused together about what each of our numbers might be. It created a helpful context for us to have some deep conversation about who we are.

More recently, I've attended several trainings with Suzanne Stabile, as well as having an opportunity to work on a number of Enneagram books with Suzanne, Ian Cron, Alice, and others. What I say here is largely shaped by their teaching. I start the sequences of reflection with the number Eight in keeping with the pattern of organizing by triads described in *The Road Back to You.*

I am grateful to my Facebook friends who offered some of the ideas that follow here about what bugs them and what makes them happy. This is of course a radically simplified list. No doubt most of these things can bug any of us at some point or another!

The images and ideas here are not meant to put anyone in box. As a matter of fact, some of the things that bug us relate to ways that we can feel stereotyped by our number. The goal here is to see how the Enneagram can help us to identify and understand the things that frustrate us. As you read through the comments from the friends who offered me their input, you may think of your own family and friends. The Enneagram can help us to be kind to one another, as well as ourselves, through a deepened understanding of how we see the world differently from one another.

8 The Challenger: Injustice. Eights react swiftly and strongly when they see powerful people doing harm to those who are weaker. They can also feel bugged by their tough reputation. Vicki says, "I feel frustrated when people assume that I will be harsh or overbearing rather than patient and caring."

9 The Peacemaker: Messes. Nines often like a tidy physical space. They can be frustrated when others choose to stay angry. Feeling pressed to make a decision for a group. Stephanie says, "As a Nine, it *really* bugs me when people tell me I can choose something, like where to go to eat, and then when I decisively answer and am feeling so proud and powerful for it, they switch to something else thinking I won't care. I do love to go with the flow because I usually truly don't care, but when you empower me to make the decision, I really care about wielding that power!"

1 The Perfectionist: Errors. People who don't follow the rules annoy Ones. As do rules that are dismissed or don't hold true. And being told to chill out. But what bugs Ones the most is their own failures. Lisa says, "As a One, people assume that I'm judging them. But I'm really judging myself harder than anyone. I don't expect perfection from others, but I want it for myself."

2 The Helper: Feeling neglected. Twos are hurt when believe that friends and family aren't putting them first. Sensing that people don't like them also hurts Twos. As does feeling unappreciated. Jacci writes, "Now that I'm aware of my Two's shadow side, it bugs me to see it in others . . . like helping when not asked to or being controlling."

3 The Performer: Not getting things done. People and processes that slow them down frustrate Threes. Threes crave independence. Robert lists some things that bug him: "Questions on a process after I've painstakingly explained it. Lack of clear direction or effort that ended up being wasted because of poor planning. Needless complication."

4 The Romantic: Being misunderstood. Feeling like they are too much for others to handle is common for Fours, which then leads to shame. Events or places that don't live up to expectations. Fours want others to know what they need without having to ask. Jason says, "It bugs me when people say, 'Cheer up' when I'm feeling murky."

5 The Investigator: Lack of personal space. Being asked to do too many things for others. Mundane conversation. Fives are frustrated by people who act like experts but are not. Suzy described such an incident: "Not long ago a person was teaching a workshop on a particular writing genre and not only was he unpublished, but he had not finished a book in this genre. He had only read a how-to book on the genre. It drove me crazy!"

6 The Loyalist: Concerns about safety. Sixes struggle with feeling they will let others down. Elaina says that people who have blind faith or a "Pollyannaish" attitude are annoying to her. At the same time, people who refuse to think proactively about the future bug them. Holly says that while she knows she tends to worry, "I hate being called a 'worry wart' or 'nervous Nellie.' To me, I'm just being practical and realistic."

7 The Enthusiast: Expectations and demands. Too much to do and not enough time to relax. Being perceived as shallow. Jessica notes, "As a Seven it bugs me when people inadvertently kill my dreams/shoot down my ideas by asking too many 'how' questions. I likely won't pursue most of the ideas I share, but I'd like people to dream with me for a minute."

When we are on the high side of our Enneagram number, living in our true self as God made us to be, it's easier to get in touch with what brings us deep and lasting joy—not the fleeting comforts we

The Enneagram and What Bugs You

seek when we are on the low side of our number. Learning the Enneagram can help us to focus on the things that bring us joy.

THE ENNEAGRAM AND WHAT BRINGS YOU JOY

8 The Challenger: Making things right. Being able to help someone deserving. Vicki finds joy when others "feel safe and welcome with me." She says, "Eights can be kind and approachable!"

9 The Peacemaker: Nature. Feeling at peace with everyone and everything. Stephanie says, "I love yoga and other forms of meditation and how calming and centering they are. Especially if I can do it while enjoying nature."

1 The Perfectionist: Order. A clean house, an organized office. Learning to make a new dish step by step and having all the ingredients on hand. Michaela mentions that she loves traveling with others to a place like Disneyland with an agreed-upon schedule. An itinerary makes it more fun for a One.

2 The Helper: Presence. Twos are happy when the people they love give them attention. Twos also want to be affirmed and appreciated for the things they do for others. Cynthia says she loves it when her adult children come for dinner.

3 The Performer: Being noticed. Getting something important done and receiving affirmation for good work is important to a Three. Joaquim felt pleased when he was able to take action to cover and protect the hyacinths in his yard when a late snow came.

4 The Romantic: Beauty. Noticing feelings. Space for creative work. Time for reflection. Fours love to learn new things about themselves and gain insights into their connection with God. In contrast to Joaquim above, Paulette says of an unexpected spring snow, "I can spend hours gazing at the scene, enjoying the heaviness of the snow on a delicate flower."

5 The Investigator: Solitude. A little time to read and think. Fives love to learn something new—just for fun. Rachel says, "I love being alone in the house because I don't have any part of my brain devoted to awareness of the other person/people. No possibility of intrusion. Somehow I feel so much freer to think and be."

6 The Loyalist: Relaxing. Feeling secure and confident. Safe and trusting long-term relationships. Alisse says that she loves "plans that work out and come together perfectly."

7 The Enthusiast: Adventures. A chance to try a new activity or eat at a new restaurant. Travel and sightseeing. Sevens know how to play! Michelle says, "Any adventure brings me joy. The crazier the better. I think international travel is probably The Best Thing Ever."

> "You mustn't wish for another life. You mustn't want to be somebody else. What you must do is this: 'Rejoice evermore. Pray without ceasing. In everything give thanks.' I am not all the way capable of so much, but those are the right instructions."
>
> WENDELL BERRY

WHAT ABOUT THAT HOUSE?

In a spiritual direction session with Marilyn I mused about what I could and should learn from the sequence of events regarding the house.

After five months on the market, we came to the conclusion that the lack of a master bathroom was the biggest reason that we weren't

PRACTICE: ENNEAGRAM TRUTH

If you know your number, take a look back through your lists over these past weeks. How does what you have recorded relate to what you know about the lows and highs of your number?

How can you be more kind to yourself in light of what you notice?

Where do you need healing or practices to pull you back from the lows?

How could you make space for more of the things that bring you joy?

getting offers. Our brilliant new realtor, Carl, helped us to figure out how to create one out of a small bedroom, while adding walls to then replace that bedroom with a slightly larger one. And our speedy and resourceful contractor, Vinnie, completed the project in a matter of weeks. Then we ran an Airbnb while we continued to market the house, which helped pay the bills. We were able to close on the house in January, nine months after we first listed it.

We knew there had been many graces in all that had transpired— including the season in which we had sold the house. We got the offer the day before Thanksgiving, not a time when people are generally trying to move. But still I often found myself wringing my hands over it all.

I'd had some sense that there was something that we could do in the new house—some way that God might use it to serve others. However, that thing wasn't becoming clear. Was I wrong to move?

Should I have not pressed into buying this particular house but waited so that we wouldn't have had the anxiety of the double mortgage? The second-guessing was still plaguing me.

We were sitting at the kitchen table in my new house. Usually we met at a little local restaurant or at Marilyn's house, but today this had worked out well for both of us. It was the first time I'd shown Marilyn the house.

The kitchen is one of my favorite spots—open and looking into a wooded area. Well-trafficked bird feeders sit outside the bay window.

Marilyn reminded me, as she often did, that God gives us space to make our own choices. It's not about the one right or wrong choice. The key is to offer all that we have to God and to see what God wants to do with it. Her input, as always, was pointing the way toward deepening self-kindness.

Then the cat let out this terrible wail. Our seventeen-year-old cat had taken up this habit of standing aimlessly in various rooms and crying. I said, "But see how unhappy the cat is. He never did this before. I've even messed up his life."

Marilyn said, "Maybe he would have started doing that anyway."

12

I DON'T HAVE ENOUGH TIME FOR THE THINGS I WANT TO DO

Finding Time for What Nourishes Us

1. What's bugging you? _Wasting time on bad TV._ _ _ _ _ _ _ _ _ _ _ _

2. What's bringing you joy? _Making more time to read._ _ _ _ _ _ _ _ _ _

As I've become more aware of the things that bring me joy, I have discovered some longings surfacing within me. For example, I'd like to have more time to garden or to have lunch with a friend or to walk at the arboretum.

When I asked some friends what bugs them most day to day, my retired editor friend Dan said, "The stack of books I'm not getting to read." For those of us who thought we were going get to read all those books in retirement, I guess that's a wake-up call.

I, too, have a stack of books on my nightstand and another pile on my desk and more on the floor by my reading chair and still more on the table next to the couch. I wish I had more time for reading.

I recently came across an article in *Flow* magazine about reading retreats. A reading retreat is a weekend away in a lovely bed-and-breakfast type setting when strangers come together to read books. The host, Cécile Wilbers, is a "literature coach." (Why didn't I ever hear about this job at career day?) She offers one-on-one sessions in which she gives recommendations for future reading. The attendees talk over dinner about favorite books and what they are reading. But mostly it's a weekend away with no responsibilities, dedicated only to reading.

Writer and podcaster Erin Straza creates her own annual beach retreat, taking along a stack of books and dedicating time to read each day. She adds in an hour of contemplative prayer practice as well.

Both of these approaches sound amazing. It's also interesting that so many of us are finding it so difficult to get to do what we want to do that we have to schedule time away to get to read a book. How can we make more time to read during an ordinary week?

WHY ARE WE WATCHING TV?

Right now I am suffering from a *The Marvelous Mrs. Maisel* hangover. I loved it so much—the storyline, the great actors, the surprising twists, and the costuming! Watching that series with my husband brought us both joy. But now I am at odds for what to watch next. So I spent twenty or thirty minutes trying to figure out what to watch next on TV. Why am I so desperate to find something to watch when I've got a pile of books that I really want to read in nearly every room of the house?

Why am I wasting my evenings on TV? It's a question I remember taking to Marilyn in spiritual direction one time. She asked me to quantify the time. And, well, I realized by the time I finished work, made dinner, tended to my kids and any other chores, it was only an hour or two of time. And I was tired. So she encouraged me to have compassion on myself with this. Some evenings an enjoyable show is a gift and a way to rest.

My TV-watching boundaries are different from those of other members of my family. I don't like violence. I don't like any sort of torture. I am drawn into some reality shows, but I know that watching them doesn't really bring me joy or refreshment. It's about numbing out and viewing other people's "made for TV" chaos. So more often lately, Dan and I agree to turn the TV off and read a little.

When Spencer was about five, we had an interesting conversation about the practice of reading. He had some views about how people should organize their reading: "You need a book to read at breakfast. Then you need a book in your backpack to read during school. And you need another book for bedtime. So you would be reading at least three books."

I like to have several books to draw from in my morning reading—ideally books with short chapters or sections. I read a bit from one or two of them. And then I just sit for a bit. Or journal a little. I began this practice when Spencer was small. I would go sit at my bedroom window, overlooking the bus stop at our corner. I'd see him get on the bus. Then I would enjoy a few moments of solitude before heading off to work, grateful that I didn't have to enter the school drop-off line. It was a great time for a little slow reading to fuel me for the day.

READING AS A SPIRITUAL PRACTICE

When I read *A Wrinkle in Time* by Madeleine L'Engle in the fourth grade, I remember something stirring within. I sensed that there was an important God message in that book. I was encountering the power of story to reveal spiritual truth.

As an adolescent I remember feeling challenged to act with courage when I read *The Hiding Place* by Corrie ten Boom. Reading Maya Angelou's *I Know Why a Caged Bird Sings* was part of what prompted me to look at going to Wake Forest University, where I was eventually able to take a class with her. In my freshman year at Wake Forest, a course called "Faith and Imagination" introduced me to the works of C. S. Lewis and J. R. R. Tolkien for the first time. They have become fast companions.

As I walk through my house and gaze at my bookshelves, I can re-create a life of reading, and of being shaped and formed by books.

Savoring. I made this collage as a reflection of my love for words and the experience of reading and writing as well as the simple joy of being surrounded by books.

PRACTICE: A FORMATIVE READING TIMELINE

When you think about the sources of your own spiritual growth and knowledge, what books come to mind? Take some time to make a list of some of your most important books—the ones that have shaped you and stayed with you. You might try making a timeline through your life and looking at key books in different eras. What are the qualities of the books and authors that are most important to you? What can you see taking place in your own spiritual development as you look at the list?

Richard Foster has been a great advocate for getting people into the great spiritual classics. Renovaré, the ministry he founded, has an online book group experience that allows people across the country and the world to connect and read together. In the introduction to the book *Devotional Classics* that he edited along with James Bryan Smith, he quotes Jean-Pierre de Caussade: "Read quietly, slowly, word for word to enter the subject more with the heart than the mind. . . . From time to time make short pauses to allow these truths time to flow through all the recesses of the soul."

The invitation to read slowly is a message we need now more than ever. And yet it was in the 1700s when de Caussade wrote about the necessity to stay with slow reading in his classic *The Sacrament of the Present Moment:* "When you find that your mind wanders, resume your reading and continue thus, frequently renewing these same pauses."

Reading for spiritual formation is not about the number of pages covered. It's about what we take in. It's about connecting with God through the writer and finding a deep moment of insight, affirmation, or renewal.

ENJOYING OUR MEALS

I've been reading *A Year in the Village of Eternity* by Tracey Lawson. It's an account of a town where the traditions of growing, harvesting, and eating fresh food are kept close to the style of many generations past. And the longevity, happiness, and health results are remarkable. I was drawn in by this passage about pasta making.

Once, this was the only way. To mix your hen-fresh eggs into fine-ground flour by hand; to knead and knead till the two become one; then to roll and roll until the yellow sheet is so spare that the sun shines through it as you lift and flip in the early light.

Watching Natalina work her fresh egg pasta, it's incredible to think that at one time this ritual was played out in every kitchen here, almost every day. Once for lunch, perhaps again for dinner, on a cold winter's evening.

I got so inspired that I went out and bought a special Italian flour at Williams Sonoma and made pasta from scratch one Sunday. I had the time to work slowly and methodically. And it came out pretty well. It was a perfect Sabbath rest experience—cooking inspired by reading.

Another part of enjoying food is to consider the way in which we consume our meals. In many retreat centers, meals are taken in silence so that participants can stay focused on what they are experiencing with God. These meals are usually set in a space where there's a nice window to gaze out of. I find it a companionable experience of being with others in the presence with God. For me it's also an opportunity to notice what I am eating—and how I am eating. I tend to gulp it down, but in a leisurely setting I am reminded to go slow. When I eat slowly, I notice the flavors more powerfully. The first bites give the strongest flavor profile to our palate. And when I eat slowly, I notice more readily when I am getting full.

Try eating slowly and silently—alone or with others—as a way to become more aware of what you are taking in. And as a way to offer gratitude for the food that you have—whether a simple meal or an extravagant one.

A TWENTY-MINUTE DETOUR

Chapter one explored the idea that time spent outside is healing. Living a suburban life of driving from a garage to a parking lot, it's important for me to get outside.

Children often encourage and motivate us to get outside. When my son was young, trips to the park with him when I'd put away my phone could become times to play or pray or reflect.

For a recent birthday, I treated myself to an arboretum membership. I can take guests at a discount, and it supports a local space where people can enjoy nature and animals can find a safe habitat. When the weather's nice—or even decent—I try to get out of the office early enough to take a spin around the pond there.

One other way I've found that I can grab a little time outside is to find stopping points at parks or walking paths on the way to or from work. I stop and take a twenty-minute walk. I look for new routes home that might allow me to discover a nice walking path.

It's just a twenty-minute detour. And it brings me joy.

> "In a way nobody sees a flower really. We haven't time. And to see takes time."
> GEORGIA O'KEEFFE

PRACTICE: WHAT WOULD YOU LIKE TO DO?

What would you like to do? Consider musical interests: When's the last time you sang in a choir? It's a great way to reorient the brain away from what's bugging you. What about opportunities to be outside more regularly? Or to either see or make art? Could you take a community college class? Or a cooking class? It's energizing to learn something new.

Return to your list of joys. Are there hobbies or activities that bring you joy that you'd like to have more time to do? What changes could you make to give yourself more time for them? What could you eliminate? Try to resist just saying, "It's impossible." Consider what you might say to a friend who told you of something they longed to do but couldn't find the time for. If nothing comes to mind, then ask God to show you a way. It might be helpful to discuss with a spouse or friend who knows your schedule as well.

EPILOGUE

What's Bringing You Joy?

Woven through these pages is the story of my experience of spiritual direction with Marilyn Stewart over a period of seventeen years. Spiritual direction is an experience of companionship in which one person comes alongside another so that they might listen for God's voice together. Throughout our time together, she helped me learn to identify the patterns of desolation and consolation in my life.

The gift of having her as a spiritual director carried me through the seasons of separation and divorce, of single parenting, and then blending families. She guided and counseled me in my editorial work as I developed spiritual formation books with many of the authors found in these pages. These experiences laid the groundwork for this book.

In my darkest moments Marilyn was like a mediator connecting me with God.

Marilyn died December 1, 2018. The meeting in my new home that I described in chapter

> *"You are the fire that takes away the coldness, illuminates the mind with light, and causes me to know your truth."*
>
> CATHERINE OF SIENA

PRACTICE: FIND A SPIRITUAL DIRECTOR

Consider seeking a spiritual director for yourself. Meetings are once a month, and most directors offer a sliding scale of fees so that it's accessible to all. Directors can be found at retreat centers and through Spiritual Directors International at sdiworld.org as well as through Evangelical Spiritual Directors Association at graftedlife .org. You might also be able to find a director through your church denomination.

eleven turned out to be the last time we met for direction. I am so grateful to be able to remember sitting with her at my kitchen table that day. She had a stroke as a result of brain cancer just a month later.

I wrote this poem to honor Marilyn and the work of spiritual direction in my life. But it also honors the movement of the Spirit in my life as I have sought to grow closer to God through spiritual practices.

The Dance of Spiritual Direction

For Marilyn

Director
Mother
Companion
Guide

When I was lost and confused, God gave me Marilyn,
and she assured me the way would be revealed.
"The path is long, but the road is broad."

When I doubted my own worth,
she pointed me to Scripture.
"You are my witness, and the servant I have chosen."

When I asked questions,
she reminded me to set them before God.
"How are you praying about that?"

When I wondered if God would act,
she spoke of God's goodness.
"God will always find a way to redeem it."

She delighted in my
spiritual progress.
She challenged my indulgences.
She called out my gifts.
She savored God's graces to me.
She pointed to the power of
Word and liturgy.
She made my world a little
more safe.
She helped me to become
my true self.
She took me by the hand and
led me into the great dance.

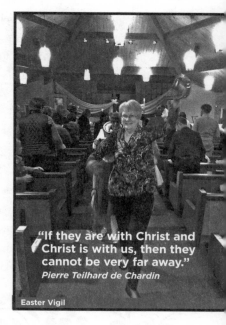

"If they are with Christ and Christ is with us, then they cannot be very far away."
Pierre Teilhard de Chardin

Easter Vigil

Marilyn's gifts to me did not end after her death. A little more than a year later, Marilyn's husband, Doug, invited some of her directees and friends to choose a few books from her personal library. Holding these books and reading through the places she had underlined or added a small "Amen" felt like being guided by her again. One of these books, *Paying Attention* by William A. Barry, SJ, spoke to me about how we find lasting joy.

Barry writes about the concept of union with God. This is the one source of true, sustaining joy. And yet he observes that we resist the very experiences that draw us close to God. He notes a common pattern in spiritually mature people in which they have a powerful, moving experience of closeness to God but then pull away from it after a period of time. He writes, "Could this be it then, that what we most deeply yearn for we most deeply fear? We fear the loss of self in surrendering to God" despite the truth that "the closer we are united with God the more ourselves we are." His answer to this dilemma? Just keep returning to God and asking for God's help to stay present. Taking note of what's bugging you and what's bringing you joy is one way to notice where you are and aren't connecting with God.

At the beginning of this journey, it was the question of what's bugging me that I found most compelling. I needed permission to uncover and name the concerns and complaints that were filling my head. I needed to identify the things—people, events, tasks—that were pulling me away from God. That remains true on a daily basis.

My new spiritual director, Jeanie Hoover, recently encouraged me to take some time in our session for whining. I needed to take that time to uncover the spiritual and emotional space in which I found myself that day. Then—as she promised—she guided me out of my whiny pit and back to God's offer to be present with me in all the things that were bothering me. If you want to make a spiritual practice of forty minutes of whining for yourself, I encourage you to try it out—especially if you have a trusted friend or spiritual director as a companion to bring you back from the whiny zone.

The other part of my journey has been noticing that God's gentle invitations are the good path that's always open to me. God doesn't offer any of us a life of ease, but God's love sustains us and holds all things together. And signs of grace are near each day.

I've continued to write down what's bugging me and what's bringing me joy each day. When I offer God the things that are bugging me and accept the daily kindnesses God offers me, I find rest.

It is so fitting that the photograph of Marilyn earlier in the chapter is an image of her leading the dance at the Easter Vigil. That night at church she grabbed my hand and brought me along around the room to sing and celebrate the risen Christ.

Joy awaits. Will you join the dance?

ACKNOWLEDGMENTS

I've edited books for many years but have never made a goal of writing one. I just wasn't sure I'd have enough to say! I surprised myself by finding enough words to fill this little book. That I was able to do so is a tribute to all that I have learned from my parents and siblings, my spouse, and my children.

As an editor, I gain riches from the authors I rub shoulders with and learn from as they let me engage their words in very tender stages of formation. I am grateful for every author I have worked with over my career. Some of their words of wisdom have found their way into these pages. But even more of their wisdom has influenced and shaped my spiritual life.

I am also thankful for my creative group friends—Cindy, Deb, Rebecca, Ruth, and Sally—who always believe in me and have been a sounding board throughout the writing process.

Eighteen years ago I had the privilege of editing the first edition of Al Hsu's very fine book *Grieving a Suicide*, which came out of a painful time in his life. It's such a gift that he could serve as my editor for this book. I have now experienced his well-honed editorial skills from the authorial side of the table and have benefited from the insight he brought to the project. After twenty-five years of working together, he's able to understand what I am trying to express but also to show me where I need to expand and clarify for the reader. As a result of his input, the book is better.

Because I work at a publishing house, I know how many hands go into making each book—and how few of them most authors know by name. I am grateful for the colleagues in every department of the building who have each contributed to this project: Jeff Crosby supported the book from the start. Lori Neff, who markets the Formatio line with the grace and kindness of a spiritual director, has taken on the daunting task of marketing a colleague's book. Ed Gilbreath keeps reminding me not to be too hard on myself. Cindy Kiple created the beautiful cover from her busy retirement studio in Mississippi. Allison Rieck offered her usual careful and kind copyediting. Jeanna Wiggins created a lovely interior design, bringing my vision to life! And I want to thank managing editor Elissa Schauer and director of production Ben McCoy, both of whom make sure our books are excellent and attractive. They make every day at work better for the rest of us. (My apologies to Elissa and Ben for the long list of names that now follows.)

Thank you to those who responded to my Facebook posts asking for input on the themes of the book relating to the Enneagram: Alisse, Ashley, Jennie, Elaina, Lesa, Jennifer, Helen, Victor, Anne, Tracey, Vicki, Suanne, Rachel, Lee, Marsha, Paulette, Jessica, Rebecca, Joaquim, Holly, Judi, Susi, Robert, Kim, Lisa, Ruth, Stephanie, Sally, Christy, Jason, Michaela, Jacci, Cynthia, Michelle, and Melodie.

And to those who commented about what bugs them and how to remedy it: Jennifer, Daniel, Valerie, Christy, Lori, Andy, Joaquim, Deb,

Debra, Claire, Kirk, Rebecca, Belinda, Matt, Jessica, Melodie, Anne, Carolyn, Suanne, Luci, Jo Ann, Kim, Dan, Christy, Shelly, Colleen, Christine, Marsha, Diane, Elizabeth, Katelyn, Bronwyn, Lee, Ava, Clare, Dorothy, Tim, Victor, Melissa, Carmen, Paula, Valeyo, Jacci, Mary, Elizabeth, Lisa, Sheila, Tish, and Margaret.

While some parts of book writing are quite solitary, I'm also struck by the ways in which other parts of the process are very communal. I am grateful for all the ways that friends, colleagues, and family have contributed to this book.

APPENDIX
The Intuitive Art Process

What follows is a slightly condensed version of the guidelines that Sheri Abel has written for a two-hour group experience.

The most straightforward way to begin is with the following supplies:

- large sheets of brown paper mounted on easels
- acrylic paints
- brushes, sponges, and various tools
- craypas (chalk)

Keep silence throughout this process.

---

1. Degunking / brain dump. 5-7 min. To help you settle in, write down in your journal the thoughts and feelings that are talking the loudest at the moment.

---

2. Intention. 5 min. Write an intention for your art making. Intentions are written in the present tense, are concrete, and in the affirmative.

Ask yourself:

- "What does my soul need?"
- "What would I like to experience during this time?"

- "Is there a mindset, a thought, an emotion that I would like to explore?"

Examples of intentions:

- "I relax"; "I play with color"; "I enjoy making art."
- "I explore my anger, my frustration, my doubt . . ."
- "I gain insight into the conversation I had with _____."
- "I receive _____"; "I'm open to receiving _____."

Release your intention to the Lord as an act of trust. You are invited to pray: "I trust you, Lord, and how you have designed my mind, body, and soul to work together. Whatever needs, wants to be expressed and/or experienced, Lord, may it be so. Let's go have some fun. Amen."

3. Art making. 1 hr. 15 min. During the art-making time, play a combination of instrumental music and world music in a language unknown to the participants, so as not to be a distraction. Music helps to short-circuit the inner critic.

It takes time for what needs to be revealed to surface. The initial artwork that we create is a way of getting ready, a type of journaling with colors and making marks on paper, thus the need to hold it loosely. It is often in the last ten to twenty minutes that a truth or thought or feeling that one's soul needs to hear or express starts to take shape.

Some suggestions to help you relax before and during the art making:

- Before you begin the art making, put on some music that has a beat you enjoy. Then start making marks on the paper with your dominant hand. After a few minutes, switch hands, and use your nondominant hand. Then use both hands. Then close your eyes. Follow your next impulse. Do you want to dance? Do you want to move your hand to the rhythm of the music? There is no right or wrong way. Experiment and see what works for you.

- Remember to breathe. The breath is grounding, and it brings us back to the present moment.

- Throughout the art-making process, give yourself permission to start fresh in any given moment: pause, smile, take a few deep breaths, and invite yourself back into the moment. Bring a quality of gentleness, regarding with kindness what arises. No judging.

---

4. Witness writing. 15 min. Witness writing is a record of an intimate moment between you, your soul, and the Lord. It is the state of being present to what you have just created and to use it as a springboard to what needs to come to the surface and be expressed.

Suggestions for your process:

Sit in stillness in front of your artwork for a few minutes.

Ask: "God, is there something here you would like me to see? To notice? Is there an invitation? Is there anything relevant between my intention and what comes up in the work? Be my guide." Then write quickly, spontaneously, without censoring or editing.

You can:

- Describe what you see
- Describe your emotional response—as you look at it now or while you were creating
- Write a story or poem or prayer in response to it
- Engage in dialogue with it—ask it a question
- Get your intention back out—what are the connections between your intention and what you see and feel here?

5. Reading and listening. 10 min. In this last step of the process, we each show our artwork. If you choose to, you can read your intention and what you wrote during the witness writing phase. You may choose to read a word, a phrase, a section, all of what you wrote, or nothing at all. Reading is different than sharing: you read without explanation, without sharing or commenting.

Reading aloud is a simple step that can take our experience to another level. When we read aloud, we blend the words of the left brain with the emotional experience of the right brain. You're engaging another sense. It allows you to hear for yourself what you wrote. What does your sense of hearing notice? What does your heart experience?

Those **listening** hold the space for the others to hear themselves reading aloud. There are no comments or questions. Comments can interfere with individuals' perceptions and feelings about their own work. Their artwork, writing, and reading are sacred moments between them and the Lord, and the listeners honor that moment. Those listening can pray silently.

The leader and group members may simply respond with "Thank you."

....

Closure. 5 min. Sit for a while in silence. Thank God for being with you every step of the process and continuing to work in your soul. Release to God the artwork and witness writing.

Witness Writing: Deb Keiser doing final witness writing with her art pieces from a six-month course

LIST OF PRACTICES

NOTES

INTRODUCTION

3   *Notice when you are bugged*: Gem and Alan Fadling, *What Does Your Soul Love?* (Downers Grove, IL: InterVarsity Press, 2019), 176.

5   *even Jesus took time away*: For more on what the Bible says about self-care and self-kindness, see Grace Liu, "What Does the Bible Say About the Self-Care Movement?" The Ethics and Religious Liberty Commission of the Southern Baptist Convention, July 5, 2019, https://erlc.com/resource-library/articles/what-does-the-bible-say-about-the-self-care-movement.

      extending ourselves to others: Anne Lamott, *Hallelujah Anyway* (New York: Riverhead, 2017), 56.

      Saint Ignatius: A brief biography of Ignatius can be found at www.franciscanmedia.org/saint-ignatius-of-loyola.

9   *Ordinary happiness is based on happenstance*: David Steindl-Rast, *Gratefulness, the Heart of Prayer* (New York: Paulist Press, 1984), 204.

      knitting gnome gif: The link to the gnome knitting gif can be found here: https://giphy.com/gifs/love-heart-valentine-3oriO6qJiXajN0TyDu.

1. I HAD A BAD DAY

20   *visio divina*: Visit abbeyofthearts.com. Also see Christine Valters Painter, *Eyes of the Heart: Photography as a Christian Contemplative Practice* (Notre Dame, IN: Sorin Books, 2013).

23   *home altar–making*: Anne Grizzle, *Reminders of God* (Brewster, MA: Paraclete Press, 2004), is out of print but available used on Amazon.

2. I CAN'T BELIEVE I SAID THAT

28   *A list can be a valuable exercise*: Marilyn McEntyre, *Make a List* (Grand Rapids: Eerdmans, 2018), 103.

What doesn't matter as much as I thought: McEntyre, *Make a List*, 106.

Inner critic as . . . terrible coach: Ellen Hendriksen, *How to Be Yourself* (New York: St Martin's Press, 2018), 99.

29   *creating for ourselves a supportive environment*: Hendriksen, *How to Be Yourself*, 100.

Some folks experience inner critics: Al Hsu, personal correspondence, July 25, 2019.

"challenging" the inner critic: Hendriksen, *How to Be Yourself*, 100.

31   *Then I turned in on myself*: Anne Lamott, *Hallelujah Anyway* (New York: Riverhead, 2017), 132.

33   *from tree to tree*: Flannery O'Connor, *Wise Blood* (New York: Farrar, Straus & Giroux, 1949), 16.

daily prayer: See www.oremus.org/liturgy/ireland/word/exa.html.

3. BEYOND MY CONTROL

35   *Sleep sound in Jesus*: Michael Card, "Sleep Sound in Jesus," *Sleep Sound in Jesus (Gentle Lullabies for Baby)*, Sparrow Records, 1989.

38   *the little indications*: Belinda Bauman, personal communication, January 23, 2019.

4. I SAW IT ON TWITTER

46   *daily morning rhythm*: Ruth Haley Barton, *Sacred Rhythms* (Downers Grove, IL: InterVarsity Press, 2006), 156.

47   *Unplugging from certain aspects*: Barton, *Sacred Rhythms*, 155.

48   *each day insults and assaults:* Sheila Wise Rowe, *Healing Racial Trauma* (Downers Grove, IL: InterVarsity Press, 2020), 145.

50   *if you use less social media*: See www.healthline.com/health-news /social-media-use-increases-depression-and-loneliness.

50   *Twitter is an anxiety machine*: *Hurry Slowly* podcast with Jocelyn K. Glei, season 2, episode 7, "Cal Newport: Using Technology with Intention."

5. RINGING IN MY EARS

57   *Thought Rhyming*: E. James Wilder et al., *Joyful Journey* (East Peoria, IL: Shepherd's House, 2015), 3.

      I see you on your patio: From a private retreat guide. Used by permission of Gayle Koehler.

58   *Follow the pattern*: The steps and Hagar references are drawn from Wilder et al., *Joyful Journey*, 36-43.

      Often we deny ourselves: Wilder et al., *Joyful Journey*, 40.

62   *God is with us*: From an Advent 2011 retreat guide for Church of the Savior. Used by permission of Doug Stewart.

6. WHEN LIFE'S ON HOLD

70   *Sleep is an act of surrender*: James Bryan Smith, *The Good and Beautiful God* (Downers Grove, IL: InterVarsity Press, 2009), 34.

76   *The more beautiful and full the remembrances*: *Dietrich Bonhoeffer Works*, vol. 8, *Letters and Papers from Prison* (Minneapolis: Fortress, 2009), letter no. 89, 238.

7. IT WASN'T SUPPOSED TO RAIN TODAY

79   *forgive or accept*: Christy Pauley, personal communication, January 23, 2019.

81   *Centering Prayer app:* See https://contemplativeoutreach.org for the centering prayer app and more resources.

      The harder you try: Martin Laird, *Into the Silent Land* (New York: Oxford, 2006), 82.

      These obsessive patterns: Laird, *Into the Silent Land*, 81.

83   *doodling prayer*: Sybil MacBeth, *Praying in Color*, expanded edition (Brewster, MA: Paraclete, 2019).

86   *It's not about skill*: See appendix for a longer version of Sheri's description of the process. First published in *Conversations* journal, fall 2016. Used by permission of the author.

8. I CAN'T BELIEVE HE DID THAT

90   *Smashing Things*: Beth Slevcove, *Broken Hallelujahs* (Downers Grove, IL: InterVarsity Press, 2016), 146.

    the concept of welcoming prayer: See www.contemplativeoutreach .org/sites/default/files/private/welcoming_prayer_trifold_2016.pdf.

91   *Welcoming Prayer:* Thomas Keating is credited as the author of this written form of the prayer. The prayer can be found on this website along with an evocative video—available free in part or in full for members: www.theworkofthepeople.com/the-welcoming-prayer.

92   *Genuine self-knowledge*: David Benner, *The Gift of Being Yourself*, exp. ed. (Downers Grove, IL: InterVarsity Press, 2015), 46.

9. I CRACKED UNDER THE PRESSURE

101   *Breath Prayer*: Adele Calhoun, *Spiritual Disciplines Handbook*, exp. ed. (Downers Grove, IL: InterVarsity Press, 2015), 233-34.

105   *I believe that what we regret*: Brené Brown, *Rising Strong* (New York: Random House, 2017), 212.

10. THINGS I DON'T WANT TO DO

109   *Learn to linger*: Sharon Garlough Brown, *Barefoot* (Downers Grove, IL: InterVarsity Press, 2016), 96.

11. SECOND-GUESSING MYSELF

113   *Know Your Enneagram Number*: Ian Morgan Cron and Suzanne Stabile, *The Road Back to You* (Downers Grove, IL: InterVarsity Press, 2016), 27.

115   *The Enneagram and What Bugs Us*: Enneagram type labels are taken from Cron and Stabile, *The Road Back to You*.

12. I DON'T HAVE ENOUGH TIME FOR THE THINGS I WANT TO DO

123 *reading retreats*: Marije van der Haar-Peters, "Reading Retreat," *Flow*, issue 27, 48-50.

annual beach retreat: Erin Straza, personal communication, May 2019. You can follow her next beach retreat on Instagram @erinstraza.

127 *Read quietly, slowly*: Richard Foster and James Bryan Smith, eds. *Devotional Classics*, rev. ed (San Francisco: Harper, 2005), 2.

When you find that your mind wanders: Jean Pierre de Caussade, *The Sacrament of the Present Moment*, as quoted in Foster and Smith, *Devotional Classics*, 2.

128 *Once, this was the only way*: Tracey Lawson, *A Year in the Village of Eternity* (New York: Bloomsbury, 2011), 45.

EPILOGUE: WHAT'S BRINGING YOU JOY?

134 *"Could this be it then"*: William A. Barry, SJ, *Paying Attention to God*, (Notre Dame, IN: Ave Maria Press, 1990), 34-35.

APPENDIX

139 *guidelines for a two-hour group*: The guidelines for intuitive art making first appeared in *Conversations* journal, fall 2016. Used by permission of Sheri Abel.

FIGURE CREDITS

Branches and Openings: collage by author

Carrying a Lullaby: collage by author

Creatures: collage by author

Easter Vigil: photo used courtesy of Al Hsu

The Enneagram and What Bugs You: collage by author

The God Who Sees Me, Palm Springs: photo by author

Hummingbird in Palm Springs: photo by author

The LORD Is Near: collage by author

I Love Doing Dishes: collage by author; photo by author of dish
    sculpture from Palm Springs Museum of Modern Art

In Need of a Shepherd: collage by author

An altar of gratitude, Palm Springs: photo by author

A template for doodling: artwork by author

Savoring: collage by author

Seeking Comfort: collage by author

Show Yourself Grace: collage by author

Time for a Reset: collage by author

Widow of Nain, 2018: artwork used courtesy of Egbert Modderman,
    www.moddermanbiblicalart.com

Witness writing: photo by author

Worlds Opening Before Me: collage by author

CONNECTING WITH THE AUTHOR

Visit cindybunch.com to view the original art in color, for printable daily examen pages, and more. You can also connect with Cindy for retreat leadership at her website.

Instagram @cindy.bunch

Twitter cindybunch

Etsy store: cindybunchbooks for self-kindness cards and other items

Cindy is a frequent contributor to the IVP *Formatio Update* newsletter. Sign up at ivpress.com/newsletters.